The
Forever
Swim

— THE OCEANS SEVEN —

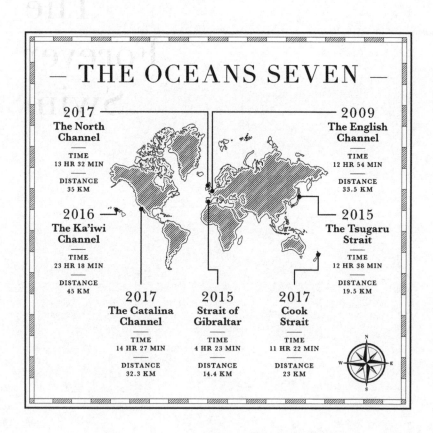

2017
**The North
Channel**

TIME
13 HR 32 MIN

DISTANCE
35 KM

2016
**The Ka'iwi
Channel**

TIME
23 HR 18 MIN

DISTANCE
45 KM

2009
**The English
Channel**

TIME
12 HR 54 MIN

DISTANCE
33.5 KM

2015
**The Tsugaru
Strait**

TIME
12 HR 38 MIN

DISTANCE
19.5 KM

2017
**The Catalina
Channel**

TIME
14 HR 27 MIN

DISTANCE
32.3 KM

2015
**Strait of
Gibraltar**

TIME
4 HR 23 MIN

DISTANCE
14.4 KM

2017
**Cook
Strait**

TIME
11 HR 22 MIN

DISTANCE
23 KM

The
Forever
Swim

ANTONIO
ARGÜELLES

EDITORIAL
REVERTÉ

The Forever Swim
First edition, 2020

Text
© Adam Skolnick, Antonio Argüelles

Photographs
© Pablo Argüelles Cattori
© María Paula Martínez Jáuregui Lorda
© Paulo Nunes dos Santos
© April Wong

Editor
Franco Bavoni

General Coordinator
Karina López

Creative Director
Ramón Reverté

Proof reading
María Teresa González

Designed by
HILL Strategic Brand Solutions – Houston, Texas

© 2020 Editorial Reverté, S.A.
Calle Loreto 13-15, local B
08029, Barcelona
reverte@reverte.com
www.reverte.com

3nd Print: February 2022

ISBN Print Edition:
978-84-291-6462-6

ISBN ebook (e-pub)
978-84-291-9563-7

ISBN ebook (pdf)
978-84-291-9564-4

Print in Spain
D.L.: B 16313-2020
Masquelibros

1510

To Shirley and Bill Lee, who adopted me and treated me like their own child, and whose affection and generosity I will never forget. The opportunity they gave me changed my life and enabled this journey.

PROLOGUE

You are about to set out, dear reader, on a fascinating journey. Thanks to this book, you will accompany Antonio Argüelles on an amazing adventure that very few human beings have dared to attempt and that only six before Antonio had completed: swimming across seven channels located in seven different seas.

A feat. An ambitious exploit. An adventure so audacious that comes close to madness and that involved swimming continuously for more than four hours in the case of the shortest crossing, the 14.4-kilometer Strait of Gibraltar, and for almost a full day in that of the longest, the 45-kilometer Kaiwi Channel. Accomplishing this feat meant enduring waters colder than the human body is usually capable of withstanding—according to the experts—as well as depriving himself of sleep for very long periods of time while performing intense physical activity. As if that were not enough, Antonio conquered this triumph at the ripe age of 58, thus becoming the oldest swimmer to complete it.

You will enjoy, attentive reader, a detailed, entertaining, and sometimes chilling account of each of the crossings that comprise the Oceans Seven, since it so happens that Toño, besides being a good swimmer, is a very good storyteller—his excellent co-author, Adam Skolnick, can certainly attest to that.

I imagine, sensitive reader, that you will suffer—as I did—in the many difficult moments, some of them almost tragic, that the protagonist of this adventure experienced as he covered such long distances in open and inhospitable waters. You will also rejoice with admiration when you read of his triumphant landings in the conquered channels, after having overcome episodes that put his physical ability, strength, and will to the test, and after having been able to find the courage not to give up and to keep swimming, literally defeating the most adverse currents until reaching the long-awaited shore.

In addition, diligent and curious reader, you will accompany Antonio in the discovery of the geography, cultures, and people of the places that generously welcomed him in each of the stages of his feat. A very important part of the story Antonio tells is what he had to do before—long before—starting each of his seven successful swims. As much as in these admirable achievements of will and physical effort, Antonio gives us a very important life lesson when he tells us how he came up with the idea of completing these seven epic feats; how he made a plan to prepare himself and how he carried it out step by step with firm discipline. Along the way, as he tells this story, Antonio walks us through the unique circumstances, dreams, and vicissitudes of his childhood, youth, and maturity.

Another great lesson is in the way in which Toño recognizes the importance of the people who have motivated, trained, and supported him in his extraordinary adventures. With sincerity, gratitude, and humility, he recognizes that his successes are also those of others, a message that is no small thing in this age of abominable narcissism and individualism.

Immerse yourself without further delay, enthusiastic reader, in Antonio Argüelles' very special journeys, because I can assure you that you will enjoy them very much.

ERNESTO ZEDILLO PONCE DE LEÓN
Yale University

Dream

When it's going well, I can feel its rhythm. The way the sea rises and falls, as I reach with my right arm, then my left, extending to my very physical limit. My legs and feet flutter and churn a wake behind me while I count the strokes that propel me forward above an abyss of inky blue.

Even with a support crew on my escort boat nearby, the hours bleed into one another, and I begin to feel alone, adrift in the channel, kilometers from my starting point, kilometers from the nearest shore. It's a longing, a beautiful kind of loneliness. Under the moonlight, in the rain, beneath a relentless sun, I swim, I sign my name in the tides.

Numbers keep me company. My stroke count occupies my brain with an endless, monotonous task. As I push my body, it's helpful to give my mind something to do. Necessary even. An unoccupied mind is a ticking time bomb, a disaster in waiting when combined with pain and discomfort: it will rebel or short circuit, like a country without opportunity.

Don't we all crave purpose? In endurance sports, especially open water swimming, like in politics and life itself, most failures are an inside job. So, I feed my mind numbers. I hand it bland tasks until it surrenders all identity, unifies around a single purpose, and I lose track of myself entirely.

Before any marathon swim begins or after it's finally over, once I've reached a destination my team and I have envisioned and worked towards for years, there's a buzz of immediacy in the air. But the swim itself feels as elastic as a dream.

A running clock ticks and tocks like white noise I can hear even in those moments when I give into the illusion, float up and out of my body high enough to peer down with a seabird's eye on the entire scene and see the truth. No matter how hard I train or how strong I feel, I'm at nature's mercy; a mere dot in a vast expanse of dark water, which swirls with currents guided by winds, and connects or divides shores and people.

Ever since I was a young boy, dwarfed by the immensity of Mexico City, riding streetcars to city pools, swimming has been my passion; that thing

I've loved over and above everything else. At various times in my life, my entire being has been shaped by swimming. I've chased Olympic dreams. I swam at Stanford University in California, and though I've worked in education and politics throughout my adult life and have run marathons, competed in triathlons and climbed mountains, it is to the water where I always return. Because no matter what else is happening in my life, good or bad, in the water I always feel free.

That's what I remembered in 2012 when I found myself towed under by the currents of life once again and woke up in a hospital bed. One minute I was at lunch, talking about climbing Mount Everest, and the next I'd slipped on the stairs, planted my foot to stop my fall, felt my leg buckle, and heard my femur crack.

During the long months of recovery, I was bored and depressed because I couldn't move. I spent six weeks at home without being able to go out, and that meant a long spell away from work. My unoccupied mind verged on rebellion and implosion, until the cast came off and I got back in the pool for the first time in three years. On terra firma, I was still limping, but in the water I was fully operational. The more I swam, the better I felt.

Then one day, after a nourishing swim at Sport City—my gym in Mexico—I ran into a good friend who told me about a new challenge called the Oceans Seven. It was created by Steven Munatones, one of open water swimming's most devoted enthusiasts and documentarians. He'd created an unprecedented challenge of seven geographically diverse channels, the aquatic version of climbing the Seven Summits—the highest points on each of the seven continents sought after by elite mountaineers.

When I got home, I logged online and the more I read about the challenges inherent in each individual swim, the more excited I became. The iconic, 33.5-kilometer long English Channel was on the Oceans Seven list, along with the 32.3-kilometer Catalina Channel. The longest was the Ka'iwi Channel, which stretches for 45 kilometers between the islands of Oahu and Molokai in Hawaii. New Zealand's 23-kilometer Cook Strait was the southern most crossing, and the 19.5-kilometer Tsugaru strait in Japan was Asia's entry. The 14.4-kilometer Strait of Gibraltar between Spain and Morocco was the shortest. Each of those six channels delivered their own particular set of hazards, including high winds, towering ocean swells, sharks, jellyfish, and busy shipping lanes, but the North Channel, which connects Northern Ireland and Scotland with 35 kilometers of frigid, dark water, was the coldest, most unpredictable, and most difficult of all.

The mere thought of swimming all over the world woke something up within me. Suddenly, my mind was no longer sluggish or surly; it was singularly focused. I ramped up my commitment and trained every day in the pool. Each weekend, I swam for hours at a time at Las Estacas, a cool, spring fed river near Cuernavaca, 90 minutes from Mexico City, and I regularly flew to La Jolla and San Francisco to taste the cold waters of the Pacific. Within a year, this was no longer a passing notion or a distant dream, but reality. In July 2015, I boarded a plane to Spain, where I would begin my quest to become just the seventh person, the first Mexican, and the oldest swimmer to complete the Oceans Seven.

Each swim taught me something vital, delivering lessons of risk, passion, adaptation, and perseverance. I learned to manage my fear and doubt and how to let go. More than anything, I learned how small I really am. How small we all are.

Often times our troubles and personal drama can feel all-encompassing, when in reality all we are is a speck of consciousness here on Earth to glow for as long as we can, like fleeting bioluminescence in an infinite sea. But as long as we are here, why not burn as brightly as possible? Why not risk everything, wake early and train hard, work your ass off all day long, drink deeply of all that life offers?

Why not swim across oceans?

Every hour of the day, all over the world, oceans relax and nourish neurotic sinners like me. They feed us and nurture all life by absorbing carbon from the atmosphere, while its phytoplankton photosynthesizes the oxygen that keeps us alive. And sometimes they hit back and brew hurricanes and typhoons of terrifying force. Oceans are all powerful, magnificent, and unpredictable, reminding us how fragile we are.

The sea—any sea—is my favorite place on Earth.

I enter and emerge at its whim.

ANTONIO ARGÜELLES

13

Swimming gives me a sort of joy, a sense of well-being so extreme that it becomes at times a sort of ecstasy. There is a total engagement in the act of swimming, in each stroke, and at the same time the mind can float free, become spellbound, in a state like a trance. I have never known anything so powerfully, so healthily euphoriant—and I am addicted to it, fretful when I cannot swim.

— OLIVER SACKS

"In each

training

session or

event, one must

become the

hero of one's

own story."

I

The English Channel

Just two hours into the most challenging swim of my life, my stomach was already twisted into knots. I was teetering on the brink. Any starlight from the moonless sky above was smothered by a cloud bank I couldn't see. I had no rhythm, no true sense of where I was or in which direction I was headed. All I knew was that I was somewhere in the North Atlantic between England and France, facing a stiff current, driven by a fierce wind.

The swells were twice their anticipated size, which made each stroke a struggle. At times I couldn't even raise my arm out of the water, and the only visible marker I could see through my goggles was a faint yellow glow from my escort boat bobbing in and out of view. It was like trying to steady yourself by locking your gaze on a yoyo dangling in space. It made me dizzy which made me queasy.

Each breath felt like a gasp between the constant waves as I strained to locate my support boat in front of me. My coach, Rodolfo Aznar, hung a lamp which he'd built himself off the stern. It was supposed to function as a guiding light, but unfortunately the yellow bulb that burned so bright on land was swallowed up by total darkness. At 3:00 a.m. my nausea spiked, and I vomited for the first time. This was a problem because I wasn't just trying to cross the English Channel once. I started in the Port of Dover with a goal to accomplish something only 27 people had accomplished before: complete a non-stop double 67-kilometer crossing from Dover to Cap Gris-Nez and back.

Up to that point in my career, I'd only been seasick once before during a marathon swim. It happened on my first attempt to swim the Catalina Channel in California. At the time, it was the most difficult and longest swim I'd ever attempted, and the boat ride out from the mainland had been rocky. The entire crew on my escort boat became ill, and I was still seasick when I jumped into the Pacific Ocean to begin the long, slow swim back toward the Southern California coast.

If you've ever been seasick, you know that it's rare to throw up just once. And each time I vomited, my anxiety boiled over because it meant I was losing energy and hydration. My body temperature began to drop. My margin of error, already razor thin, shrunk fast, and within four hours, I'd quit. The pain, the bad weather, and my illness proved too much to bear.

Now it seemed to be happening a second time, but there was something else—or rather someone else—on my mind. Her name was Fausta Marín, another Mexican swimmer who, just two weeks before, had collapsed mid-swim in the English Channel and was never revived. When she was pronounced dead, she became just the eighth swimmer in 124 years to perish while attempting to swim the Channel. Her death was major news in Mexico. She was just 41 years old.

I wasn't the only person thinking about her as I struggled to harness my energy and plow through the wind and waves. My crew was too. They watched me carefully, especially my friend and close advisor Nora Toledano. Fausta was her good friend and Nora had been with her the day she died; in fact, she was coaching her. The earliest sign that Nora had of anything going wrong with Fausta was when she vomited two hours into her swim. In other words, through Nora's eyes it looked like the wrong kind of history was starting to repeat itself.

Today, open water swimming is one of the world's fastest growing endurance sports, but back in 1999 when I stepped into the English Channel, it was still relatively obscure. Nobody paid much attention then to who crossed the Catalina Channel, and the extremists who swam around the island of Manhattan in New York City weren't celebrated for much except their sheer lunacy. Remember when Kramer took up swimming off the Manhattan piers in *Seinfeld*, the hit television show? His East River stink didn't help make open water swimming popular in New York!

But the English Channel, the first audacious channel swim to populate our cultural radar, has long claimed a special place in human hearts. Perhaps it's because the history between England and France is so loaded, or maybe it's that the thought of anybody greasing themselves up, and swimming across the North Atlantic Ocean from one country to another, while wearing just a Speedo, a swim cap and goggles, sounds as mad as it ever has.

As far as oceans go, the Channel itself is relatively shallow, but it links parts of the North Sea and the Atlantic Ocean and is one of the busiest shipping lanes in the world. It's a stretch of water that has been patrolled by Romans and the Spanish Armada, Napoleonic sailing ships, and Nazi U-boats. It has also managed to keep the English safe from all potential invaders except the aforementioned Romans and a French and Flemish force led by William the Conqueror in the 11th century (the Vikings successfully invaded England twice, but via Scotland). On the other hand, the Brits and their allies have crossed the Channel multiple times, most famously in 1944, with the U.S. invasion of occupied France on D-Day.

The first swimmer to cross the English Channel was British Navy Captain Matthew Webb, who swam breaststroke head-up between August 24-25, 1875. It took him nearly 22 hours, maybe because he was getting his hydration and energy from single malt scotch.

More than 50 years later, there were still less than ten swimmers who had managed to duplicate his feat, including one woman. Gertrude Ederle made it across in 1926. That didn't stop dozens of others from *claiming* they'd crossed the English Channel. Thus, in 1927 the first channel swimming association was founded as an official governing body to authenticate and ratify all channel attempts. They set the ground rules that almost all other channel associations now adhere to. Following the precedent of Matthew Webb, swimmers may only wear a swimsuit, cap and goggles, but unlike the Navy captain, drinking alcohol along the way for both the swimmer and crew is no longer allowed.

At the time of writing, more than 1,800 people have swum across the English Channel unassisted. But swimming 'unassisted' doesn't mean those swimmers didn't have help. It means that they were not touched by anyone along the way, and that they never stopped to hold onto the side of a boat, kayak or flotation device of any kind. Oh, but to cross the English Channel—to complete any major marathon swim— swimmers do need plenty of help.

Open water swimming wasn't even on my mind until 1996, when just two days before the 100th Boston Marathon, I tore my calf muscle during a training run. I was 37 years old and was in charge of the largest technical high-school system in Mexico: the Colegio Nacional de Educación Profesional Técnica (Conalep). I was accomplished in politics and public administration, and I'd achieved a fair bit as an amateur athlete too. I was a triathlete, an Ironman, and I once ran the New York City marathon in two hours and 55 minutes. My life had a familiar rhythm to it. I set big goals—both in work and sports—and used them to give my life shape, texture, structure and, most important, purpose. But once any of my goals were accomplished, I wouldn't spend more than a few seconds celebrating the victory before I'd sense a black hole opening up below me, driving me once again to the next challenge.

What I'm trying to say is nothing I did—no matter how well I did it—made me feel good about myself. There was always an inherent insecurity nibbling at my well-being. The setting of a new goal allowed me to momentarily ignore that existential itch, but once I'd achieved my immediate goal at hand, my sense of inadequacy always reappeared. Nothing was ever good enough. I was never good enough.

Within a few weeks that small seed—a casual, passing notion from a friend— had germinated into a dream of my own.

Laid up because of my injured calf, I felt demoralized and knew I needed to focus my attention on another objective before I drowned myself in alcohol. Just like in sports and at work, one drink was never enough at the bar. As soon as I could see the bottom of my glass, I needed to fill it up.

One day, a friend who knew my background as a swimmer suggested I swim the English Channel. It struck me as odd because in my mind I wasn't a swimmer anymore. I swam to compete in triathlons, but I spent much more time riding my bicycle and running. Since graduating from college, the longest swim I'd completed was the 3.9-kilometer swim in the Ironman in Kona. I hadn't swum more than 3000 meters in a pool in almost 20 years and I had never come close to swimming 33.5 kilometers in one shot. I told him he was crazy and told myself to forget all about it.

Except I didn't forget. I couldn't. The seed had been planted and the more I thought about it and researched the Channel's history, the more attached to the idea I became. Within a few weeks that small seed—a casual, passing notion from a friend—had germinated into a dream of my own, one I had no clue how to pull off.

My friend Alexander Kormanowski, a Russian biochemist who was one of the first scientists in Mexico to test the blood of athletes and use the findings to help them tailor their training, suggested getting in touch with Nora Toledano. Nora was just the second Mexican woman to cross the Channel under her own power. By 1996, when I sought her out, she had already done it five separate times. But what made her an international open water legend was her 1994 swim when she became just the 12th person, and first Latin American, to complete a two-way crossing from Dover to France and back. It took her nearly 24 hours. In 1996 she was still just 26 years old, and in Mexico very few people had ever heard her name, but no other Mexican swimmer—and very few swimmers worldwide—had her level of experience in the English Channel.

We met five weeks after my injury, on May 10th, 1996, on the riverside of Las Estacas. The swimmable portion of the river is not very long. It stretches just one kilometer from end to end, and the goal that morning wasn't to cover some premeditated distance. It was simply to swim continuously up and down the river for three hours without stopping.

I was nervous at first because I wasn't sure I could keep up with a legend like Nora, and if she did leave me behind, I wondered if she would still be willing to advise my team. Perhaps she was going easy on me, but I was able to keep up. Though it was a boring swim, that was good too, because there was one thing I already knew: if I was going to complete the English Channel, I was going to have to fight the boredom battle countless times. After that initial swim, we sat together on the riverbank.

"Crossing the Channel," she said, "isn't merely a matter of endurance. Swimming continuously for hours and hours won't be enough. To break through tough currents, it's important to keep up a strong pace."

She helped my coach, Rodolfo Aznar, put a training plan together, focused on my speed. We set timed goals for every 1500 meters I swam in the pool. Once a month we also did a test set to see how many meters I could cover in a full hour. I supplemented pool work with the occasional swim at Las Estacas and a lot of time in the gym to build up my back and shoulder muscles, biceps and triceps. Once my pace picked up, we scheduled a series of longer swims to prepare me for the challenge to come and to prove myself to the Channel Swimming and Piloting Federation. You are permitted to hire one of the boats (and boat captains) sanctioned by the

Federation only after your qualification swim is confirmed. Then, on the day of the crossing, the Federation arranges for an official observer to be aboard your support boat to confirm that you swim unassisted across the English Channel from beginning to end.

Qualifying meant swimming at least six hours continuously in open water at a temperature that hovers between 16-18°C. Our best option was Lake Zirahuén, a natural lake in the Michoacán countryside surrounded by green hills and pasture land that is especially lovely in the early morning. Nora and I arrived the night before our swim, and when we told the inn keepers of our intentions—that we planned on waking at 3:30 a.m. so we could swim across the lake at 4 a.m.—they thought we were crazy and almost kicked us out. After some sweet talking, they handed over the keys to the inn so we could make our exit as quietly as possible the following morning.

A thick fog had rolled in overnight. When we stepped outside, we couldn't see the lake from the shore. Visibility was three meters at the most, and the air temperature was quite a bit colder than the water, which is the only reason we jumped in and started swimming. It wasn't an easy swim, because my blood sugar was low, but my discomfort was soothed by the natural beauty. As the sun rose and burned through the fog, pine-dappled hills and golden fields appeared. The deep lake was crystalline and looked bottomless. I wasn't bored. I was mesmerized. Once we arrived back on shore after swimming six hours non-stop, I was English Channel qualified.

That was just one of eleven long swims I completed from July 1997 to July 1999 as I prepared for the English Channel. I circumnavigated Manhattan Island in New York and felt

25

energized by seeing one of my favorite cities in the world from the water. I swam in the shadow of the Statue of Liberty and up the East River where I passed beneath the Brooklyn, Manhattan, and Williamsburg Bridges, before merging with the Harlem River and swimming to the top of the island. From there, it was a long swim down the Hudson River, around the heart of New York City. I remember seeing the Twin Towers rising in the distance as I closed in on the finish line at Battery Park.

Not all of my long training swims were so enjoyable. When I swam for 12 straight hours, from 4:00 a.m. to 4:00 p.m., at Las Estacas, it was a test of my sanity more than anything. Talk about battling boredom. I was swimming the same stretch of water over and over again for half a day. In the wee hours, I had the river to myself, while at sunrise I enjoyed watching turtles swim, fish, and rest on the riverbanks. After 8:00 a.m., so many people showed up that the river became a slalom course. In the afternoon most visitors left, and the turtles went into hiding, so it was up to me to contend with mind-numbing nothingness. But once it was over, I'd learned something about patience, endurance, and my own ability to keep going long past mental and physical exhaustion.

My final adventure before the main event—the two-way English Channel crossing—was another attempt of the Catalina Channel on July 12th, 1999 (more on Catalina later). This time I made it, which meant a successful crossing of the English Channel would enable me to achieve the Triple Crown of Open Water Swimming. At the time, there was no Oceans Seven and the Triple Crown (a circumnavigation of Manhattan, and crossing of both the Catalina and the English

Channel) was the most sought-after achievement in the open water. After that twelve-and-a-half-hour Catalina swim, I remember standing on the rocky shore of California, just north of Long Beach, thinking how cold the Pacific Ocean felt that day. In July, the Pacific is nearly as cold as the English Channel, and yet I felt so good, I was more convinced than ever that I could achieve the English Channel double. But I still had six more weeks until I would be able to prove it, and a lot can happen in six short weeks.

I was in my office in Metepec, near Toluca in the State of Mexico, on August 20th, 1999, when I first heard the news. In those days we all had beepers, and I received a message from a friend that afternoon: a swimmer had died in the English Channel. I was aware that Fausta was supposed to be swimming that day, but there can be as many as five swimmers attempting an English Channel crossing on any given day. Yet when I went online and read the AP story, my heart dropped.

Fausta Marín was born poor in a rural pueblo in Mexico and came to the capital city to work and study as a young woman. She found a job as a housekeeper, and her boss quickly saw that she was bright and burned with an inner drive, so she gave her time off to study. Fausta began secondary school later than most, but graduated and then moved on to university, where she met Nora.

Though they were 15 years apart in age, Nora and Fausta became close as they studied biology and swam together for three years. Fausta was never the gifted swimmer that Nora was (very few are), and she idolized her young friend. When Nora crossed the Channel for the first time and was celebrated within the worldwide open water swimming community, a seed was planted within Fausta. Nora never formally coached Fausta in Mexico. I was the first athlete Nora had ever consulted with, but we both knew that Fausta was also training for the Channel. Given that open water swimming is an expensive sport and she was doing the best she could on a limited income, we invited her to join in some of our training swims. When she found out that Nora would be in Dover for my attempt at the Channel double, she asked Nora to act as her coach and crew chief on her crossing.

After reading the AP report, I called Nora. She didn't pick up the telephone in England, but I kept trying for hours. When I finally reached her, she was in tears. The press was all over her. News outlets from around the world wanted to know what had gone wrong. Nora told me the whole story.

Fausta was seasick from the beginning of the swim and had trouble keeping her food and fluid down. On long channel crossings, it's common for swimmers to vomit. Many swimmers will throw up at some point during a 33.5-kilometer swim. It's less common to start out feeling ill, but despite that, Fausta never looked to be in life or death distress and, true to her nature, she never complained.

By hour three, Fausta began having trouble urinating and at the four-hour mark, she changed her position from freestyle to backstroke. She was obviously uncomfortable, but discomfort is a given on any marathon swim. Her decision to abandon her most efficient stroke (freestyle) just four hours into the crossing puzzled Nora, so she called Fausta over to the side of the boat.

Nora leaned over the railing, mulling the series of easy questions she would ask to gauge Fausta's responsiveness. Until then, Fausta had been alert and communicative, and Nora knew that she'd done much longer swims before, but she was also aware that hypothermia can sneak up on a swimmer and before anybody realizes it, their mind may begin to malfunction. Simple questions enable coaches and crew chiefs to evaluate their athlete. Is their speech slurred? Are they confused? How quickly do those easy answers come?

Nora waited, but Fausta did not answer and kept swimming. She called to her friend one more time. Again, there was no response. Fausta kept hammering away, so Nora took action. She pulled off her shoes, jumped into the water, fully clothed, swam over and took a good look at Fausta, who looked to be awake but lost in a fog. She didn't even realize that Nora was swimming alongside her. Alarmed, Nora grabbed her and as soon as she did, Fausta went limp. Nora swam her towards the boat using a side stroke like a lifeguard might during a rescue, and along the way Fausta lost consciousness. The crew pulled Fausta on deck and laid her down flat. Dripping wet, Nora climbed aboard and kneeled beside her. She was no longer breathing.

The captain radioed the coast guard, and Nora and her support crew delivered CPR. It took the coast guard about forty minutes to locate them and when they arrived, they brought Fausta aboard their rescue boat, and continued CPR as they accelerated toward England. An hour later Nora and her crew landed at Dover and heard the news. Fausta was

29

gone. The cause of death was listed as pulmonary edema—a build up of fluid in the lungs, which prevents the exchange of carbon dioxide and oxygen. Pulmonary edema is like an internal drowning, and it's one of the deadliest side effects of hypothermia.

It was a horrible story to hear, let alone live through, and all I could do was try and calm Nora, and walk her through how to deal with the press. Of course, given this news I had some messaging of my own to do. Within days, my closest friends and family, especially my wife, Lucía, and my daughter, Ximena, would beg me to cancel my swim.

Among the dozens of people who approached me the week of Fausta's death was Nelson Vargas, the coach of Mexico's national swimming team, and my former coach and business partner. He asked me how I could trust someone who had lost a swimmer like that. He wasn't the only one to ask the question, but I found it unfair. Nora did not drown Fausta. If anything, her death simply underlined the inherent risks of open water swimming, something I should have always understood. Marathon swimming in cold water is an extreme sport and I shouldn't be casual about discounting those potentially deadly risks. When it came to training, I hadn't been casual at all. I'd trained hard and it was Rodolfo and Nora who had pushed and prepared me. I was in great shape and now it was up to me to remain mentally strong in the aftermath of a crisis.

I came home that night and explained to Lucía that even though I understood why she was concerned, I still had to try and swim the Channel. She didn't like my decision but accepted it. With Ximena, my daughter, the situation was much more delicate. Initially, I'd hoped to shield her from the news of Fausta's death because I didn't want her to worry; her classmates, however, made sure she heard the truth. They taunted her and told her that the same thing would happen to me. That I would die in the middle of the ocean. I explained that lightning seldom strikes twice and that I planned to make her proud.

The three of us left for Europe about ten days after Fausta's death. We flew to Paris, where we met up with Nora, and the four of us took the train to Calais on the northern shore of France and boarded a ferry to Dover. Nora had not set foot in the water since Fausta's death. So, while Lucía and Ximena checked us into our hotel, Nora and I walked down to Swimmers' Beach in Dover. That's where swimmers gather and train before they swim the Channel.

Open water swimming had made Nora Toledano a star in the marathon swim community worldwide. It had given her a career as an athlete and a coach, but now the thought of going back to the ocean terrified her. She hesitated. I took her hand and led her toward the tide line. The water lapped at our toes.

"I will hold your hand as long as necessary," I said, "and when you are ready, we will swim, and you will see that nothing will happen to us."

We were both crying as we walked forward until the water was knee high, then up to our hips. When it reached my navel, I looked over, she wiped her tears away and nodded. We began to swim. When we first arrived in Dover, she told me she didn't think she wanted to swim again, but after two nourishing hours, she was able to relax for the first time since her friend died.

A week later, I was on nearby Shakespeare Beach. It was 1:00 a.m. and Nora wasn't with me. She was aboard my support boat, the *Aegean Blue*, which idled about 100 meters offshore. There was no wind and the water in the sheltered harbor was glassy and calm. When Captain Mike Oram sounded his horn, the clock started and after nearly three years of preparation, my attempt to swim across the English Channel and back finally began.

My strokes felt powerful as I glided through the harbor and found an early rhythm, but as soon as we rounded the corner and entered the Channel itself, the swell and the current picked up, and what started out as perfect conditions deteriorated fast. I struggled to meet the moment and my form eroded. Nora watched me closely.

Although our relaxing swims in the previous days eased her mind somewhat, she still did not want to board the boat that night. She was anxious and unsure, but I told her that I needed her, and she agreed. Then for the next two hours I fought currents and swam at a near standstill as I struggled to see the boat. When I started to vomit, my mind unraveled a little further and the sicker I became the more Nora's concern mushroomed.

When I swam to the boat for fluids and food, I could see her watching me, hunting for signs of distress, wondering when—not if—I would crack. Being so sick early on in a swim is not normal, and as my most experienced advisor, I'd given her, and her alone, the power to end my swim if she felt I was in trouble, even though I knew that in the aftermath of

Fausta's death, she would not hesitate to give the order.

I kept fighting, trying to stay focused as images of Lucía and Ximena continued to occupy my mind. Before I left for the beach that night, I'd promised Lucía that if the swim wasn't going well and my health suffered, I would give up. When I said it, I felt like I meant it, but now I wasn't so sure. Maybe I would keep swimming no matter how I felt. Was I conditioned to swim until my body gave out, like Fausta? That realization chilled my bones even more.

My only hope was to quit worrying about distance and time and start focusing on damage control. I needed to stop throwing up because my energy was being depleted and even though the water was on the warmer side as far as the English Channel goes (16°C), my core temperature was dropping because I was so sick. I needed to relax my pace and gain control of my mind and body.

I slowed down and relaxed my breathing, yet my nausea persisted. Four hours into the swim, at 5:00 a.m., I should have been nearly 40% through my first crossing, and I'd just passed the 20% mark. But I couldn't think about that because my intestines were still twisted in knots. I'd been fighting the urge to expel everything inside me. I was worried it would take too long, and, given the current, I'd lose ground, but it had to be done, so I shifted to a sidestroke and dropped my Speedo.

It took a long time, but I was finally able to let everything go and my abdominal pain subsided. That's when the cold seeped in. I began shivering uncontrollably. I heard my bones rattle and felt weak. My muscles were stiffening. My skin burned. I thought I'd done everything possible to prepare myself for the cold. I'd packed on 33 pounds of muscle and fat and hadn't taken a warm shower for months. I'd completed multiple swims in water nearly as cold as the English Channel only to tremble in its grip. Fausta's face bloomed in my imagination. I told myself I was feeling everything she must have experienced. I was swimming in her wake. Negativity was dead weight dragging me down in the darkest waters.

But as dawn approached, the sky faded from dark blue to orange and finally the sun broke through. In the daylight, I no longer had to follow the bobbing yellow glow and my nausea evaporated. Still, whenever I stole a glance over at my support boat, I always spied Nora watching me closely. It was time to pick up my pace. That was the only way to warm up and instill confidence in my team and, more importantly, within me. I had to wipe all negativity from my mind. I'd put on those pounds for a reason. I'd trained my ass off, and to be successful I had to trust the process and my preparation and begin to perform at something close to my best.

It helped that I had survived the night. How many times have you woken up in the middle of the night worrying or feeling anxious about a job undone, or a love lost? In the darkness, noises and shadows become unnerving and monstrous, and if that's how it feels on land, imagine how it feels in the open water. In daylight, everything felt new and I found a rhythm, though my progress was still slow because the current was pushing me northeast. Instead of swimming in a straight line, I would have to swim an S-curve to successfully make it to Cap Gris-Nez in France.

During a feeding break, I calculated the time it would take to complete my first crossing and it was starting to look like I'd be in the water for close to 20 hours just to make it across the Channel once. It was time to shift my perspective. Five swimmers attempted to cross the English Channel that day, and by morning only two of us were still swimming—the other three had already quit—because the currents had been so unforgiving. Obviously, given the conditions, a double crossing was beyond my capability, but if I crossed the English Channel once I could still achieve the Triple Crown of Open Water Swimming.

From that moment on, I no longer cared about distance or time. I would simply swim. The only reason the clock mattered to me at all was because at the bottom of the hour I would stop to drink, at the 40-minute mark I would urinate, and at the top of the hour I would eat. That allowed me to break the swim up into small, digestible chunks, which made it manageable for my mind.

At 10 a.m., I swam to the side of the boat for a snack, but instead of just Nora or Rodolfo, all the members of my support crew crowded the railing. Roberto López Peña, Nora's husband at the time and one of the five members of my team on board the *Aegean Blue*, cleared his throat.

"Toño," he began, "you have been in the water for nine hours now and we are not yet even half way to France. We are very worried about you and have voted unanimously to pull you out of the water. I'm sorry, but your swim is over."

Furious, I threw my water bottle back on deck. Were these people blind? Yes, I had a poor start, but I was no longer sick, and my form was getting better, not worse!

"I don't know what you intend to do," I screamed at them, "but I am swimming!"

I swam off, my mind simmering with rage I used to pick up my pace, which was exactly what they'd hoped. I'd find out later that the intervention was staged to test my fire and gauge what I had left in the tank. Judging from my reaction, it was obvious to all of them that I had a lot more effort, determination, and passion still to burn. Plus, since Nora hadn't been the one to break the news her authority remained intact. The truth was, they didn't need to take a vote. Nora alone could end my swim whenever she wanted and we all knew it.

Yes, there would be so many ways and means to justify failure, but all of them—every single one—paled in comparison to the simplicity of success.

Their trick drove me forward. For the next hour, I imagined what would happen if I was forced to give up. I knew I'd hear the same questions over and over from people who don't understand the power and capriciousness of nature.

"How did you fail?" They would ask. "Did you not train enough? When will you try again?"

Ximena's friends at school would mock her, of course, and my pride would be bruised. Plus, with all my work commitments (I had 262 schools to supervise), finding the time, not to mention the sponsorship, to stage a second attempt would be near impossible. I had one chance and I had to push ahead. I had to finish!

I remembered a line from a George Sheehan essay in *Runner's World*. "In each training session or event," he wrote, "one must become the hero of one's own story." That's all I thought about with every stroke. Within an hour, I hit the halfway point and the current shifted. Suddenly it was at my back pushing me onward. It felt to me like I'd scaled a peak and was now swimming downhill. In Mexico, we have a saying: even pumpkins can roll downhill.

I thought of all my achievements in sports. On my 40th birthday, I'd swum across the channel from La Paz to Espíritu Santo. It took me 12 hours and if I could do that once I knew I could do it again. When the 12-hour mark came and went I flashed back to the 1995 Ironman in Kona, which took me 13 hours to complete. I knew I could duplicate that effort and then some. I was also gaining energy from my nutrition. From the eighth hour on, I was enjoying treats like grapes and melon, and from the tenth hour, I began sipping beef broth, which warmed my body and soul and infused me with energy.

With a favorable current behind me, I chewed up the kilometers and soon the French coast appeared in the distance. Roberto shouted that I was less than eight kilometers from shore. I knew from experience that if I kept my current pace, I could make that distance in two hours, which would put my crossing at roughly 15 hours. Not a bad time considering how it all began, but within seconds, a new reality hit me in the form of a stiff wind that kicked up to 14 knots. The tide shifted again too. Suddenly I was being pushed north, away from Cap Gris-Nez. That's how fast conditions can change in the open water.

Like a bad dream, I could see my destination, but no matter how hard I swam I could not inch any closer. Another boat buzzed towards us. It was the support boat for a Brazilian swimmer I'd met in Dover. He was the fourth swimmer to abandon the Channel that day. I was the last man in the water, the last man still fighting the fates, and the always unpredictable ocean.

Swimming in place with the wind-swept waves crashing on my head, I cataloged all the excuses I might use for my failure: Fausta's death, my illness, the currents, the winds. I'd tell everyone that I was the last swimmer to give in to nature, the toughest of all the swimmers in the English Channel on its worst day. That could provide some solace, I thought. Yes, there would be so many ways and means to justify failure, but all of them—every single one—paled in comparison to the simplicity of success. Once again, I had to stop the negative stream of consciousness. I had to manage my thoughts.

I started to imagine how good it would feel to reach the French shore and with that vision firmly entrenched in my mind, I focused on my breathing and visualized a jet stream propelling me forward despite the wind. Within a few minutes, I found a rhythm and the determination I needed to compete with Mother Nature, but she would not relent.

During my feed at hour 17, Roberto gave me more bad news. We'd been pushed off course from Cap Gris-Nez. There was another sliver of beach that could work as a landing spot and that was our new destination, but he warned me:

"The captain says that if you don't increase your rhythm and make it to the beach in the next two hours, we will be pushed wide again, and you'll have to swim another three to four hours to the next beach."

I'd been swimming for 17 straight hours, which had earned me three options: go as hard as I could for as long as I could and hope for the best, be conservative, stay steady and preserve my energy for a five to six-hour swim, or abandon the swim entirely.

It was an easy choice. I dug deep, channeled all my passion, and increased my pace from 62 strokes per minute to 68 strokes per minute. Inspired by my effort, my team cheered me on, shouting encouragement until they grew hoarse. Their energy gave me life and I went even harder. Within an hour, I had broken through the oncoming current that faded as I closed in on the French shore.

I knew landing would be tricky because we missed the sandy beach at Cap Gris-Nez. This "beach" was nothing more than a jumble of slick boulders, studded with sharp shells, at the base of high bluffs. After swimming for so many hours, I didn't want to end up splattered on those rocks, so as I drew closer, I slowed down to adjust to the rhythm of the waves.

I let them lift me up and drop me onto smaller boulders. From there, I crawled onto a big rock to satisfy the rule that required me to clear the water completely. I tried to stand, but my legs were jelly and I could not. Still, I was out of the water from head to toe, and when Captain Oram saw that he sounded his horn. I raised my right hand and pumped my fist. After a swim of 18 hours and 19 minutes I became just the 12th Mexican to successfully swim across the English Channel. More than a physical feat, this had been the most intense mental challenge in my athletic life. I'd come face-to-face with defeat and overcome all the obstacles.

I swam slowly back to the boat, climbed aboard, and walked straight to Nora. Before we left, I'd dedicated the swim to Fausta and after enduring some of the worst conditions the Channel could offer, we embraced with tears in our eyes.

My legs were still wobbly from being horizontal for so many hours and as I staggered to the stern of the boat, Roberto shook my hand. "You've conquered the Channel," he said with a glint of victory in his eye. I laughed and threw my arm around him as the Captain wheeled us back toward Dover. Then I turned toward the horizon where I could see the English Channel spread out in all its power and glory. One does not conquer the English Channel, I thought. If anything, I was fortunate to be allowed across.

Lucía and Ximena met us on the harbor in Dover. It felt good to hold them in my arms and see them so relieved, relaxed and happy, but that night and for several nights to follow, I couldn't sleep at all. Adrenaline thrummed through me; I was anything but relieved or relaxed.

CHAPTER ONE

In fact, for months afterwards, I was lost. I couldn't make any sense of my accomplishment. Was it real? Was it a dream? Was it just another meaningless event lost in the past forever? I knew only one thing for certain. I had no plans to make another crossing like that ever again. I had already achieved the Triple Crown of Open Water Swimming, after all. There was nothing left for me to seek in the open water.

With tears in my

eyes and a fire in

my belly, I knew, for

the first time, what I

wanted to do with my

life: I wanted to be

an Olympic swimmer.

2

Passion

Whenever the *organillero* turned his crank in the old center of Coyoacán, I could hear its airy whisper. His carnival melodies floated up and out of his weathered pipe organ, until the breeze caught them and carried them down tiled alleyways, and walking streets, through the trees and our open windows like an interloping spirit. On quiet afternoons, I could hear his wobbly song from blocks away. It was an alarm telling me the streets were about to come alive. That it was time to go outside and enjoy the last shards of sunlight. On this one particular late afternoon, I made a wish as I rushed out the front door of my parents' house and looked up. The sun had dropped below the mountains to the west, and the sky was turning pink.

Although Mexico City sits at 2,250 meters above sea level, Octobers in Coyoacán are warm into the early evening.

Vendors gather on street corners hawking steamed sweet potatoes, pork tamales, and *elotes*; cobs of yellow corn pierced with a stick, pulled from a bubbling pot of water and spiced and sauced with lime, chile and cheese, just as they did when I was an eager nine-year-old boy in 1968. Back then on the typical autumn evening, I would follow the *organillero's* song and those aromas to the buzz of the Coyoacán *zócalo*, where even more vendors gathered, before joining my father on house calls around the neighborhood. This wasn't a typical night, however. Not in the slightest. The Olympics were in Mexico City that year and as I sprinted through the tiled streets, the world's lens had zoomed in on a shiny new pool complex built for the occasion.

Both my parents were veterinarians. During the day, my father sold pharmaceuticals for pets and livestock and my mother was a researcher at the National Autonomous University of Mexico (UNAM). At night, my father ran a clinic out of our house with the occasional house call mixed in. I used to love making house calls with my dad. There was a Doberman here, a Persian cat over there, and the occasional chicken clucking from its courtyard pen.

The animals were owned by the painters and actors, writers and professors who were our neighbors. This was the neighborhood that Frida Kahlo made famous, though she died before I was born. Gabriel Figueroa—a famous cinematographer, perhaps Mexico's finest from Hollywood's golden age—was our most celebrated neighbor during my childhood. Miguel León Portilla, a distinguished historian, Pablo O'Higgins, a famous American muralist (a contemporary of Diego and Frida), and Manuel Álvarez

Bravo, the most famous 20th-century Mexican photographer, lived nearby too. We were surrounded by all manner of bohemians and intellectuals. And compared to them, we, the Argüelles family, were rather square.

Still I heard our neighbors talk. During the summer and fall of 1968, heated opinions floated through the streets as often as the *organillero's* song. Activists were meeting in neighborhood houses, organizing and planning their next demonstration in what came to be known as the Mexican Student Movement. I didn't comprehend much at the time, but I understand now. Though Mexico's economy had performed fairly well during the previous three decades, with sustained growth and little inflation, there was simmering discontent among certain sectors of the population, particularly students. Paralleling movements in Paris and Berkeley, they called a general strike, gathered, and marched for free speech and increased accountability for police and military units, and to voice their anger at prolonged authoritarian rule.

Protests made governmental authorities uneasy, especially as the Olympic Games drew near. The Olympics, scheduled for mid-October, were supposed to be an opportunity for Mexico City to take the world stage and demonstrate that Mexico was, in fact, an emerging economy. Oh yes, we do love our illusions.

With pressure rising to complete Olympic venues like the swim stadium before the Games began, the regime acquired a habit of suppressing demonstrations with force. But that didn't deter students from continuing to organize: marches, clashes, and riots did not stop.

It all came to a head on October 2nd, when a multitude of university and high school students gathered on the Plaza de las Tres Culturas for a public demonstration. Just before sundown, the gathering was buzzed by helicopters, which was nothing new, but this time red flares came raining down from above stirring up chaos in the crowd.

Snipers perched on rooftops began picking off protesters, and when troops moved in from tanks and trucks with orders to disperse the crowd, some opened fire on the unarmed students. What began as a peaceful protest became the Tlateloco Massacre. Though there is no official count, dozens, maybe hundreds, of activists were killed and arrested by soldiers and police. After the last bullet had been fired and the final body hauled away, the nation mourned.

All this fear, rage, and tragedy went over my head at the time. All I knew was that my dad went down to the university, which had been occupied by the military in an attempt to shutdown organizers and activists from plotting more protests, with his small, secret agent camera he'd bought as a joke. Like a low budget James Bond, he snapped photos of the occupation for posterity's sake.

Ten days later, the Olympic torch was lit.

For the first week, my brothers and I would take the bus to the Olympic Village and ask athletes for autographs. I loved everything about the Olympic atmosphere: the countless cultures and languages, the international spotlight, and the strength and glamour of the athletes. We didn't have a television at my house back then, but I refused to miss a thing. At night, I would visit my grandparents and together we would watch the Olympic Games.

The Summer Olympics in 1968 would be remembered for so much. There was American Bob Beamon's world record in the long jump, and the famous protest when American sprinters Tommie Smith and Juan Carlos gave the black power salute while their national anthem played. They were expelled from the Games. But in Mexico what we remember is that 1968 was the most successful Olympiad in our history. Mexican athletes won nine medals altogether: three gold, three silver, and three bronze.

Mexico had never won an Olympic medal in the pool prior to 1968, but we had high hopes going into those Games thanks to a swimmer by the name of Guillermo Echevarría. He had set the world record in the 1500m freestyle at the Santa Clara Open—a major swim event in northern California—prior to the Olympics. Thanks to all the hype around Echevarría, he became my hero. Unfortunately, he failed to even make the final in the 400m freestyle (his other event). Then, on the biggest stage, with an entire nation tuned in and the Mexican President himself watching from the stands, Echevarría entered the pool venue and stepped up to the starting blocks for the 1500m freestyle.

The gun sounded. He shot out fast and grabbed the lead but couldn't hold it. He faded as the laps piled up and finished in sixth place, nearly a full minute behind the gold medalist, American Mike Burton. Echevarría's Olympics were a disaster, and it looked like Mexico would remain also-rans in the pool, as usual, but as the swimming events drew to a close, an unexpected Mexican swimmer emerged with a chance at history. His name was Felipe Muñoz.

That's what drew me into the streets and away from my father's house call rounds that Autumn evening. I didn't follow the *organillero* to the *zócalo* and ignored the alluring aromas that caused my stomach to rumble and my tongue to sweat. Instead, I sprinted three blocks to my paternal grandparents' house.

Televisions weren't a common appliance in Mexico in 1968, but my grandfather was a buyer for Sears, and their 24-inch black and white RCA was the best one could get in Mexico at that time. It was encased in a polished wooden cabinet and when you turned it on, like I did after rushing through the door, a beam of light sprouted from the tube and expanded into a full picture.

It revealed the pool in all its glory. Olympic banners hung from the rafters, the crowd buzzed, and eight athletes stretched on the blocks in the 200m breaststroke finals. My grandmother and grandfather each had their own favorite chair in their living room, facing the TV. They looked as delighted as I was, but not nearly as nervous. I kept shifting in my seat on the sofa. Standing, sitting and fidgeting, frothing with energy.

Even when the Olympics weren't on, my grandparents' house was a haven for my brothers and me. It's where we played marbles and with a set of 200 toy soldiers. I was a hyperactive kid and sometimes we played both at the same time. It was my grandmother's idea to use our marbles as weapons to mow an opposing army down.

Their bookcase was an armchair traveler's dream, stuffed with Spanish and English language literature. The reason my grandfather landed the job with Sears was because he attended high school in the United States, where he learned English, which made him something of a rarity in mid-century Mexico City and a valuable commodity for any American company looking to penetrate the Mexican market. I never forgot that, probably because his high school yearbook from the United States was in that bookcase and he was constantly showing it off.

The camera framed young Felipe. I stood and hopped up and down. *"Dios mío, Toño,"* my grandmother said, *"¡tranquilo!"* But she knew I couldn't stop the electricity from pulsing through me as the athletes grabbed the handles below their starting blocks, and coiled, set to launch into the water.

Muñoz had the fastest time during qualifying the day before and was swimming in lane four, but he wasn't the favorite. American Brian Job and Russian Vladimir Kosinsky were the more celebrated and accomplished swimmers. Nobody expected the baby faced, 17-year old Mexican to deliver a repeat performance and steal the show in the final.

Whether or not he learned any lessons from Echevarría's mistakes in the 1500m final is anybody's guess, but when the gun sounded, Muñoz did not race to the front of the pack. He was at least two body lengths off Kosinsky, and in fifth place by the time the athletes reached the second turn at the 100m mark. That's when the 17-year-old flipped the switch.

He moved through the water with grace and force. As he drew closer to the Russian and the American, the energy in the crowd gathered like a brewing storm. He made the turn at the 150m mark in third place and the crowd stood and began yelling his nickname in unison.

"Tibio, Tibio, Tibio!"

I was hopping up and down, chanting along with the crowd. My grandparents were leaning so far forward, they were in danger of falling over. We watched as Muñoz caught Job, then glided past him. On the last lap, he drew even with Kosinsky. The Russian refused to yield, but with his last stroke and glide, Muñoz managed to out-touch him and the sold-out arena exploded, celebrating an Olympic gold!

His teammates rushed to the pool deck, lifted Muñoz into their shoulders, and paraded him around like a conquering hero. I bounced on the sofa and ran around the room as if I was celebrating along with them. But when he took the podium, the gold medal was placed around his neck, our flag was raised and national anthem played, I stood still, tears in my eyes and a fire in my belly. That's when I knew, for the first time, what I wanted to do with my life. I wanted to be an Olympic swimmer. I wanted to taste that competition, camaraderie, and glory for myself.

My mother's father, Diego, had a pool at his house in Cuernavaca. He was a veterinarian too, and an officer in the Mexican army. He came to his rank, and his wealth, in an untraditional way thanks to a former president and his beloved horse.

Manuel Ávila Camacho, the last general to rule the Mexican republic, had a ranch in Cuernavaca and was known as a great horseman and polo player. My grandfather grew up poor, one of 13 children, and enlisted in the army to seek a better life. In the service he studied veterinary medicine, became a lieutenant, and was based in Cuernavaca when the then president's favorite mare grew ill with Celiac disease, which is fatal in horses.

Yet no matter how rough the days were at school, my troubles vanished when I hit the water. Swimming became my outlet for pent up stress, and it gave me much needed confidence.

The army dispatched my grandfather to Ávila Camacho's ranch where he spent all night caring for that mare. My grandfather was terrified of what might happen should the horse lose its life, but by morning, the horse was out of danger. Relieved, he humbly packed his medical bag, left the ranch, returned home and slept all day and night.

When he heard the news, President Ávila Camacho sent a telegram to the Minister of Defense saying that my grandfather had earned a promotion to Lieutenant Colonel, bypassing several rungs on the ladder of hierarchy including Captain and Major. Imagine going to sleep a mid-level officer and waking up in an entirely different stratosphere. That's a great night's sleep.

In the 1940s, Cuernavaca was the inland version of Acapulco. It was picturesque, known for its foreign residents—most of them American—and my grandfather's good deed earned widespread exposure. He built a robust private practice that did so well that by the 1950s he'd started buying property, including a sprawling ranch, where he raised pork and grew tomatoes for market.

As kids, our parents took us to my grandfather's house on the weekends year-round, and after Muñoz won his gold medal, I would swim laps in his pool twice a day even though it wasn't that long, was much deeper than a real lap pool, and was never heated. Even the cold couldn't dissuade me. But my imagination was a poor facsimile of true competitive swimming, and I was hungry for the real thing.

In those days, you had two options as a youth swimmer. You either joined a private club or you went to the public complexes, which included day care centers, pools, and gyms. Public facilities were quite good, but too far from Coyoacán. My mother eventually opted for enrolling us in the pool program at the Coyoacán YMCA, a fifteen-minute trolley ride from home. It was another expense for the family, but my mother could sense that swimming was more than a fleeting interest for me and agreed to make an effort to pay the fees if I promised to improve my grades and stay out of trouble at school. At the time, I was falling behind in school and couldn't harness my attention long enough to study, let alone retain any knowledge of the material. I accepted the deal and it changed my life.

I was ten years old when my brothers and I started swimming at the bottom rung of the Mexico City youth swimming ladder. Our YMCA team was considered—and was—third rate and we competed against a lot of other third-rate teams around the city, which allowed me to pile up victories. My brother Raúl did well in his age group too. Based on pure talent, he was as good or even better than I was, and our other brother, Diego, joined the water polo team.

Swimming was without a doubt the best thing in my life because school was a pain in my ass. My mother was convinced that a good education was the best gift she could give us. She knew, from her own experience, all the disadvantages of not speaking other languages, and that a good, multilingual education required enrollment in one of the best private schools in the city.

We attended the German School where for the first three years we were taught in both German and Spanish, then in fourth grade they integrated an English curriculum. By my fourth year in school, my brothers and I were on our way to becoming trilingual, which sounds terrific now, but that kind of intellectual pressure can be difficult on a pudgy, hyperactive kid who didn't feel very good about himself.

I was heavier than most kids, which made me a target, and I couldn't remain on task, no matter how hard I tried.

During first, second, and third grades, I didn't sit still for more than fifteen minutes at a time and was constantly out of my seat, bouncing around the room looking for attention and learning next to nothing.

I had trouble with numbers, had difficulty with grammar and spelling even in my mother tongue, which resulted in bad grades, and when other kids ridiculed me for my weight, I got into fights on the playground. The school complained to my mother who would scold me. Thank God, attention deficit disorder and hyperactive disorder were not buzzwords yet, so nobody tried to put me on medication. My teachers' theory was that eventually I'd grow out of it, and I would have to, or they wouldn't let me attend one of the city's best schools past sixth grade.

Yet no matter how rough the days were at school, my troubles vanished when I hit the water. Swimming became my outlet for pent up stress, and it gave me much needed confidence. During my first year at the YMCA, I broke personal best after personal best, and the daily exercise soon pacified my mind and stretched my attention span, as it physically exhausted me. I developed focus and determination and I grew to expect success both in and out of the water.

The German School system in Mexico City was a school district all its own, with a handful of primary feeder schools and one secondary school. The pressure was on during sixth grade, because only fifty percent of all the children attending German primary schools would be allowed to continue their education in the German School system in seventh grade. I was studying harder than ever, but still wasn't a shoo-in. My main motivation was the secondary school's glittering 25m pool. They had a wonderful athletic program and I wanted to be part of it. I knew this because during sixth grade, when I was just 12 years old, I got my first taste.

Each year, there was a swim meet between all the best swimmers in the German School system, called *Schwimmfest*. I was thrilled to be able to compete and as I stepped onto the pool deck, I was dazzled by the plaques drilled into a wall running alongside the pool: The Wall of Records. I vowed to break them all. But first, there was the matter of winning my age group as a sixth grader. It wasn't even close. I blew everyone away.

The following Monday, the teachers read my name out to the class and raised the Mexican flag. When we sang the national anthem together, it felt like a junior version of my Olympic dreams had manifested, but my happiness wouldn't last. I never competed in that beautiful pool again.

I didn't miss the academic cut. In the end, my teachers pushed me just enough to make it, but the day I brought home my acceptance letter to my parents, my mother told us that we were transferring to the Swiss School, which was ranked a bit higher in academics, had smaller class sizes, and was closer to Coyoacán. That meant leaving that Wall of Records and all my friends behind.

The Swiss School was everything I knew it would be. Dull as hell, and full of frowning students and teachers who were all straining so hard to be proper and do everything perfectly, there was never any room for fun. There was no passion. I felt out of place and unmotivated. It didn't help that I was still mired on my third-rate YMCA team. Even at that age I knew I needed to step up my training and coaching if I hoped to make the Olympics.

One afternoon I found the upgrade I was looking for thanks to a classmate whose mother was good friends with Mr. Echevarría, the father of the Olympian and one-time world record holder, who managed the Olympic Pool. After the Olympics, the competition pool became a public resource for lap swimmers, and its caretakers built a competitive youth program, which included swimming, synchronized swimming, diving and water polo. Their coaches were superior to those at the YMCA, and the facilities were top notch, so I crossed my fingers and went down to the Olympic Pool to ask Mr. Echevarría if I could join the team.

I did not look the part. I was pudgier than the typical elite swimmer, and I could tell that Mr. Echevarría wasn't impressed as he looked me up and down. He didn't hide the fact that he doubted my ability, but was willing to give me a shot.

"To swim with us, you'll have to practice twice a day. In the morning and the afternoon," he said. He went on to explain that I needed ten pesos for a physical exam, another 50 pesos to join the team and I'd need to find an additional 30 pesos per month to train there, which was money I didn't have. With three kids in private school, and another on the way, my parents weren't likely to be excited by a steeper bill to pay.

Without even mentioning it to my parents, I woke up at 5:00 a.m. the following morning and made my way back to the Olympic Pool by trolley for 6:00 a.m. practice. On most swim teams, athletes are divided into groups with the slowest swimmers gathered in lane one and the fastest in lane eight. When I arrived, the coaches didn't ask for my times in the 100m freestyle or any other stroke. They directed me to lane eight and bunched me with the very best guys on the team. It was my trial by fire.

Most of the others were better swimmers than me. Some were already on the national team and they didn't exactly welcome me with open arms. In fact, once training started, they took off fast and left me gasping as I swam all out to keep pace. I fell back almost immediately. As they made the turn at the 50m mark, I took elbows on my shoulders and my jaw from swimmers who were on their way back to where we had started. I had to turn and try to draft in their wake. I swam 80 meters for their every 100, all morning long. Afterwards they all laughed at me. Even the coaches were hoping that I would quit.

I felt inferior in every way, but I didn't give up, and when I look back, I always think of having to overcome that inferiority. It wasn't easy. After I returned home from my long workouts in the pool, my mother (who I'd told about switching to the Olympic Pool after that first session) would always ask how I was feeling, if I was making progress and enjoying myself, but I couldn't tell her, my father, or my brothers the truth. That each day was another humiliation, another opportunity to be ridiculed and feel defeated.

For weeks it went like that. I turned up eager to learn, ready to work, perfect my stroke, and swim harder than ever, only to have my nose rubbed in the fact that I didn't measure up to kids who were stronger, leaner, meaner, and more confident than I was. The harder I tried, the louder they would laugh when I failed.

One evening before I went to sleep, I lingered in the bathroom and stared at myself in the mirror. It was time to choose. Would I succumb to the negativity conspiring to suck me under, and quit, or was I willing to channel my passion, find another gear, and rise above all the bullying and ridicule? I made a promise to myself that I would do whatever it took to improve, and that someday, I would lead lane eight.

Twice a day I made the trek to and from the Olympic Pool. I left the house before dawn and got home after sunset. I was swimming close to ten kilometers per day and the entire process had me worn out. I fell asleep at my desk at school almost every morning. Other afternoons I skipped classes altogether, but by the end of my first season swimming with the Olympic Pool team I had caught up with the lane eight leaders and was prepared to represent our club in the 400m freestyle at the Mexico City championships.

58

To win the city championship, I didn't just have to beat all my teammates, but swimmers from the Social Security team, as well, which was the most elite swimming program in the city. The director of the Social Security team was Nelson Vargas, and he prided himself on recruiting the best swimmers into his program. In fact, he bought them with a small stipend. Instead of having to pay for coaching or to have access to a pool, his swimmers got paid, and he employed the very best coaches in Mexico.

I knew all of this, of course. Everyone did, which is why winning the city championship meant so much to me. I had to show them who I was and what I could do. I needed that stipend because my father had just lost his job. That meant my mother's salary would be stretched thin. We barely had enough to pay for our schooling. Extra pesos to chase my

Olympic dreams were out of the question. I needed to find that other gear and win, or I could forget about swimming for a while.

I climbed to the blocks in lane six for the final. I was the third fastest qualifier but coming in third this time wouldn't solve my problems. I had to win. When the gun went off, I dove in and took off. From the second I hit the water, my heart thumped hard. My lungs heaved. My passion bubbled to the surface and I wanted to show everybody just how fast I was, but I knew from watching Felipe Muñoz all those years ago, that as much as I wanted to go all out, I had to muffle my initial thrust and lurk in the middle of the pack. I saw shadows and splashes on either side of me, and tracked the race leader, biding my time until the 200m turn.

That's when I went nuclear. I couldn't feel or hear a thing. I was in tunnel vision mode, all pain and flow, giving it everything I had. I built up a body length lead by the time I turned for the final 50m. With just one pool length to go, I swam with desperation and passion. Technique went out the window as my competitors charged after me, trying to track me down. They ran out of room. I out-touched the runner up and won the race by a few tenths of a second.

I was city champion! Moments later, I stood on the podium to receive my medal, and as I bent down I remembered Felipe Muñoz. I was still a far cry from his pinnacle, but I'd taken another modest step, at least.

As predicted, before I left the pool, Nelson Vargas called out to me from the bleachers as my teammates gawked, still shocked by my victory. They saw us shake hands and knew what that meant. I would soon join Mr. Vargas' team.

I'd made some good friends at the Olympic Pool and had been happy there in the end, but it was time to move on again. Not just because of the stipend, which while helpful, was only enough to cover transportation to and from the Social Security pool where we practiced twice a day. The real reason I wanted to join Nelson's team was his sporting goods business, which he operated out of his office at the pool. He sold Speedo swim caps, goggles, and swim suits—and I wanted a piece of that action.

The pool was on the northeast side of town, in a crime-riddled neighborhood, almost as far as you can get from Coyoacán. At first, my mother would wake up with me at 4:00 a.m., drive me to practice, and wait there until 7:00 a.m. when she would drive me to school. After school, we made the same trek across town, but it wasn't long before that ritual exhausted itself.

Our mother was our only bread winner and driving that much hampered her ability to earn extra money. My father wasn't even making house calls like he had in the past. There were school fees for four boys, utilities, and transportation expenses. I knew my mother couldn't carry all that weight alone. She tried though. She started making her own pet food and selling it door to door, but that wasn't nearly enough. I needed to pitch in.

One day after practice, I approached Nelson and told him that I could help sell his swim goods in the southern end of the city. He was intrigued, because he didn't distribute to pools in and around Coyoacán, and offered to increase my stipend to a small salary. I shook him off. I told him that the only way this new arrangement would work was if I could buy his stock at cost and sell it myself for a small profit. Nelson was dubious, but he agreed to supply me with ten sets of swim suits, goggles, and caps to see what I could do.

In those days, it was difficult to get anything made abroad in Mexico. We had a closed economy. There were only a few options of any product available in stores, and we didn't have international-grade sporting goods manufacturers operating domestically. Translation: our stock was better than consumers could get anywhere else.

I spent that next weekend visiting every pool in and around Coyoacán and southern Mexico City. All of them had small kiosks where they sold whatever meager swim supplies they could get their hands on. Very few had any swim suits at all, and each of the kiosks not only bought what I already had but ordered even more. When I reported back to Nelson, he seemed impressed and again offered me a salary, but I'd already run the numbers. I told him I wanted to be his lead distributor for the entire city and that we could split the profits, 50-50. I also mentioned that we'd need more stock. He laughed.

"My contact at Speedo can help with that," he said.

By 1974, when I first started swimming for Nelson, Speedo had only recently become a big name in the swimming world. Founded in Australia by a Scottish immigrant in 1914, it wasn't a well-known brand in international swimming until the 1968

Olympics in Mexico City when 27 of the 29 gold medalists in the pool were wearing Speedo swimsuits. 1968 is also when Nelson first met Bill Lee, an American businessman who loved swimming and had just licensed the Speedo brand from its Aussie owners to sell their wares in the U.S. and Canada. A few years later, in the early 1970s, Speedo patented their sleek elastane (spandex) fabric and began making swim suits out of it.

The rest is history. Their athletes broke records by the dozen at the Munich Olympics in 1972, and from then on almost every serious swimmer all over the world wanted to be in Speedo gear. But because Mexico was a closed economy, Bill Lee couldn't crack it until Nelson came up with an ingenious solution.

Our team was the best in Mexico, and we'd visit the U.S. for swim meets in Texas by bus. Nelson and I would divide up our small shipments from Bill Lee, which we picked up at the Texas pools, and ask each of the swimmers to pack a handful of items in their luggage. Upon our return to Mexico, it was my job to collect the stock and sell it.

I couldn't manage swimming, school, and all the sales and inventory on my own, so I brought my brothers, Diego and Raúl, into the business. As I mentioned, Raúl was a competitive swimmer too, and Diego was a water polo player, so whenever we had a swim meet we'd compete, but we also opened our own pop up sporting goods shop and spread out the swim suits, caps, and goggles on a towel for everyone to peruse and purchase. I went everywhere with swim suits, goggles, and caps. Swimmers and their parents called me the bag man because I never went anywhere without two suitcases. The beauty of our business model was that there was no competition because nobody else in the country was selling Speedo.

The biggest challenge was transportation, but in those days you only had to be 15 to drive in Mexico, and even though money was tight, my mother took out a loan from my grandfather Raúl to buy me a red VW beetle to celebrate my 15th birthday. I used it to cover nearly 100 kilometers every day to train and attend school, and to earn money for the family. That car became our office, stockroom, and delivery van all in one.

Trouble was, the Social Security team trained in a rough barrio and several of my teammates came from poor families. They saw the cash I carried thanks to our sporting goods business, and noticed I was one of Nelson's favorites. Some resented me for it. When I turned up at practice in my new car for the first time, several of my teammates hinted it would get stripped or stolen while we swam. One day, one of the kids on the team approached me with anger in his eyes. He said I'd hit him on the head during a flip turn.

"After practice," he said, "you're gonna pay!"

I faced a dilemma. On the one hand, I was not a bad fighter—I had a brown belt in judo—but I did not want to break the promise I'd made to my mother about staying out of trouble. On the other hand, I knew that if I ducked my teammate, there would be no end to the bullying. I'd be taunted and picked on relentlessly, and my car would be trashed, if not stolen outright. It came down to a simple choice. Show up and fight or quit the team, and if I did that, I'd lose the business that my family was beginning to rely on.

As I mulled my options, another teammate approached me. His last name was Denicia, a tough kid who came from the neighborhood where we trained. Everyone feared him, even the bully who challenged me. But instead of threatening me, he asked me for a favor. He said that if I let him be my roommate on the next trip to the US, he would handle my troubles within the team and make sure nobody touched my car. Near the end of swim practice, he approached me again, this time in the deep end of the pool.

"Don't go in that locker room," he whispered.

"I have to, or I'll never have any respect here," I said.

"Listen to me," he said, pressing a firm hand on my shoulder, "if you go in there, I can't protect you and you will take a vicious beating. Just go. Don't bother showering. Okay? And after today, you won't have any more problems. I promise."

I nodded, and when Nelson's whistle blew, I did as Denicia asked. I grabbed my gear from the side of the pool and slipped out undetected. When I returned to practice the next morning, nobody hassled me and my bully had a black eye of his own.

Why did Denicia defend me? Because I could speak English, and that meant I could help him buy things his family needed on our trips to the United States. In the border towns we visited, it was easy to find household appliances, name brand clothing, or even better brands of candy, which were next to impossible to find even in Mexico's biggest city due to the closed economy. Denicia's mother had always sent him to the border meets with a shopping list, but he'd never had the courage or the language skills to buy what she needed, which caused him problems at home. Helping him was easy for me and we became very good friends.

I had twin passions: swimming and business. On the swim front, I focused on improving my time in the 400m and 1500m freestyle, which were my best chances of making the national team. Meanwhile, the Speedo business was going so well, I no longer relied upon Nelson to provide all the capital to buy our stock. I'd earned enough money to kick in capital as well, and on every trip to the States, we brought home all the gear that we needed. Our orders were so big that Bill Lee took notice. I would place our orders with him over the phone, but I hadn't yet met him face to face, and he didn't know how young I really was.

That October in 1975, the Pan American games were held in Mexico City. Though I was still very young, I trained hard hoping to make the national team. After all, if Felipe Muñoz could win an Olympic gold medal at 17, I felt I could make the Mexican national team—not the greatest national team in the world—at 15, and compete at the international level for the first time. In the weeks leading up to the Pan American trials, I put in the work. I'd swim six kilometers in the morning and put in a full ten kilometer workout each and every afternoon.

School was the last thing on my mind. Although I did well in the core subjects, I was failing three classes. I was a disaster in music—I couldn't read sheet music to save my life—and German, and I was even failing P.E. I was preparing to try out for the national swim team but couldn't pass high school gym class.

The Pan American trials were held in the Olympic Committee pool and I was prepared to compete in three

65

events: the 200m freestyle, the 400m freestyle and the 1500m freestyle. Only the top two were guaranteed a spot on the team, with the third-place finishers slotted in as alternates.

I wasn't a contender in the 200m and came in fifth place. When it came to the 400m and 1500m events, I felt confident and strong. Nobody in Mexico trained as hard or as long as me, and though my competitors were between two and four years older, I felt I could win.

In the final heat of both events, I led the race until the very last lap. In the 400m, I built a big lead in the third 100, but unlike during the city championships, I couldn't hold it, and was out-touched for second place by one one hundredth of a second. That made me an alternate, meaning I wouldn't be able to compete or be a part of the team unless one of the two men ahead of me had to pull out due to injury. The 1500m race played out the same way. Again, I led the race for a substantial portion, and gave up the lead in the final 50m. I finished in third place twice. I may as well have come in last. I was a two-time alternate.

Nevertheless, as I showered and dressed, I felt more hope than dejection. I'd come so close at just 15 years old, I felt I had a legitimate chance to make the Olympic team the very next year. Plus, our swim business was flourishing. We were making a lot of money and Bill Lee was thrilled that Speedos were available in Mexico. Before I left the locker room that day, I flashed to our last call together.

"I'm very impressed with what you guys are doing in Mexico, Antonio," he said. "Very impressive growth. I know a lot of that is because of your effort."

"Thank you, Mr. Lee," I said, in the deepest baritone I could muster. He still had no idea how old I was.

"It's the truth, and I look forward to meeting you face to face soon enough," he said. "In fact, I wonder if you could arrange a driver for me when I come to Mexico for the Games?" I couldn't help but smile. There were so many reasons to remain optimistic.

"Of course, Mr. Lee. I know a very good driver."

The Pan Am Games were held in early October. I met Bill Lee at baggage claim where I was surprised to find him wrestling with ten boxes of Speedo gear. Up until then, I thought he understood why we picked our shipments up in the US, and I didn't have a plan to shepherd so much merchandise through customs. Odds were, all of it would be held or subject to steep duties and he would want to know why.

We stacked the boxes and I told Bill to wait, while I went over to speak with the customs officials. I didn't know what to tell them. I was just 16 years old, way out of my element. Then, just as I was about to extend a hand and introduce myself to the customs officers, fate stepped through a sliding glass door in the form of the great Felipe Muñoz, the official ambassador of the Pan Am games in 1975.

"William Lee!" He bellowed. "*¡Bienvenido a México!*"

They shook hands and, with a nervous smile plastered to my face, I pulled Muñoz aside. He had duty free stickers in his pants pocket to help VIPs get their personal belongings through customs with minimal hassle. I asked for ten of them.

He looked at me, confused. I gestured toward Bill's boxes. He nodded, pressed them into the palm of my hand, and without the customs officers noticing, I stuck them to each box that Bill brought in from the United States, then wheeled them right out the door. Bill watched as I loaded them into the back of his waiting van.

"So, you're my new friend, Antonio," he said. "That was quite a trick you pulled off with customs, young man."

"Yes, Mr. Lee."

He laughed, patted me on the back, climbed into the van along with the American water polo legend, Andy Burke, and off they went to their hotel.

Bill and Andy booked rooms at the Camino Real Hotel—a midcentury modern architectural jewel in the Polanco neighborhood built by the great architect Ricardo Legorreta—for the full two weeks of the Games. On his first night in town, the Lees and Burkes booked dinner at Bill's favorite restaurant, San Ángel Inn. I was told to have his driver greet him downstairs in the lobby at 8:00 p.m. sharp. I agreed, but 8:00 p.m. came and went and Bill was nowhere to be found. Finally, at 8:30 pm, he and his wife, Shirley, and Mr. and Mrs. Burke appeared. Bill was surprised to see me. Instead of shaking my hand, he looked me up and down, clearly disapproving of my attire. I wasn't dressed like a typical driver. I was in jeans and a white button down.

"Pretty casual get up there," he said. I looked down at my jeans and Converse sneakers. In Mexico, wearing Levi's and a pair of Converse implied a certain status, because both were unavailable in Mexico. Bill didn't get it. To him, I looked like a punk kid. After a moment of hesitation, he motioned for me to follow him out the front door. "Okay, let's go. Do you know where San Ángel Inn restaurant is?" I hustled after him.

"Of course, Mr. Lee."

"Good," he said and stepped toward a waiting town car.

"Ummm, this way, Mr. Lee," I said as I led him to my VW beetle, parked behind the Lincoln. He stopped short and stared at the car. Then he glanced at his party of four, trying to work out the physics. I smiled and opened the passenger door.

Andy nodded and folded his 6'3" 220-pound frame into the tiny bucket seats in back. Their wives followed suit. Bill Lee sat shotgun and after closing the passenger door, I ran around the back and settled into the driver's seat. I started the car and looked over at Bill who stared off in the distance, annoyed. Well, that made two of us because I had been waiting for 30 minutes.

"I'm sorry, Mr. Lee, but I have to say something. I was here at 8:00 p.m. and you kept me waiting for 30 minutes." He looked over shocked.

"Excuse me?"

"I was waiting for you for 30 minutes."

"Well, you're Mexican," he said, "and in my experience, Mexicans are always late."

"Well, I'm not. You should know that by now," I said. "Please don't do that to me again." Mr. Lee glared at me for a moment, then smiled.

"I'm sorry, Antonio," he said. "It won't happen again." I put the car in gear, and we rolled toward the driveway which spilled onto a bustling four lane boulevard.

"You know, when I saw you at the airport, there was so much going on I didn't see how young you are. You've been pulling off this whole business, and you're what, 17 years old?"

"Sixteen," I said with a sharp nod. Caught somewhere between shock and respect, he laughed as I revved the engine, zipped into a gap in traffic and accelerated towards the restaurant.

"I love Mexico!" He shouted.

For the next two weeks, I shadowed him wherever he went. His goal during that competition was to make sure every athlete on the podium was wearing Speedo in the water. That meant befriending coaches and athletes from across the Americas. Obviously, he knew the entire roster of U.S. swimmers personally, but I found it more impressive that he had a decent grasp of Spanish and cared about meeting the Latin American and Caribbean athletes too.

From what I could tell, Speedo meant everything to Bill Lee and it made sense. He started with a small licensing deal and built an obscure Australian brand into an American marketing powerhouse. His first move had been to sell to kiosks and vendors at neighborhood pools in California, just like Nelson and I were doing in Mexico, and at the Pan Am Games he was the man, known everywhere as Mr. Speedo.

As I drove him to the airport after the closing ceremony he peppered me with questions. I told him about how I'd narrowly missed making the Pan Am Games and shared my Olympic dreams.

"Are you happy with the coaching here?" he asked.

"Nelson Vargas is the best we have in Mexico."

"I know that, but... I just think." His voice trailed off. After a few moments, he gathered his thoughts. "You are

70

a gifted young man, Antonio, and I would like to see you achieve your dreams."

I was still so young I couldn't grasp what he was trying to communicate. I didn't yet know about the California swim culture, their competitive clubs—like the famed Santa Clara and De Anza Swim Clubs—and had very little clue about the top level coaching I was missing out on. All I knew for sure by the time Bill Lee stepped out of my beetle, grabbed his suitcase from the curb and shook my hand, was that I had made a good friend.

For the next six months I was all about training hard and working towards the Olympic Games in Montreal, held in the summer of 1976. By then, the business I built with Nelson and my brothers paid for all of our school fees and more than compensated for my father's financial issues, but it was draining. I had no time for anything but training and work, and was often caught napping at my desk at school.

Yet, with the business thriving, I was on the phone with Bill Lee several times a month and he kept tabs on my training. At one point, he suggested I reach out to a friend of his in Dallas, Skip Kenney, a famous American swim coach. I called several times, but Skip never returned my messages, and I had no choice but to place my faith in the training program I already had.

As the Olympics approached, I was still ranked third in the country in the 1500m freestyle, and felt I had a decent shot at making the team. But once again I failed at the trials, missing the team by ten full seconds. I'd regressed, but that didn't dampen my passion for the sport. After all, I was still only 17 years old.

I did end up going to the Montreal Olympics. Nelson brought me along as his guest. We met Bill Lee there who gave us tickets to all the swim events and showed us around the new Speedo warehouse in Montreal, as well. Though I'd promised Bill not to scalp the tickets he gave me, I couldn't resist selling them to make some good money on the side. Not that he knew anything about it.

Once again, all the Olympic champions wore Speedos, but it was hard for me to watch the swimmers because my passion to compete was so strong. Mr. Lee sensed my turmoil and one evening made me an offer that would alter the course of my life.

We were sitting in the VIP room at the Olympic Pool before the night session was set to begin. He was on top of the swim world at that time, so it felt good to be part of his inner circle. I'd never asked him for anything but swim goods before, which we'd paid for, and felt the time had come to ask for a favor.

"Mr. Lee, I feel like I'm stuck," I said.

"Stuck how?"

"I've plateaued. I'm not getting faster and feel I need better coaching. The kind we can't get in Mexico. I tried to call Mr. Kenney, but he never returned my messages. Would you be able to call one of the swim clubs in the States and ask them to accept me next summer?"

He turned toward me but didn't respond right away. He had a way of seeing through me that felt very paternal. His eyes lingered on mine before he finally nodded and lifted them toward the window, overlooking the immaculate pool deck.

"Well, of course I can do that, but why wait until next year?"

"I have school," I said. "I have to wait."

"I understand that, but…" He took a deep breath then turned to face me one more time. "I've spoken to Shirley about it, and we would like you to come live with us. You could finish high school in Los Altos and swim with the De Anza Swim Club."

My heart skipped. I wasn't sure I'd heard what he said accurately. Was I dreaming? Could he be serious?

"How much would I have to pay?" I asked, hesitantly. He smiled.

"No, Antonio. It would be… it would be as if you were our son."

In those few seconds I swore I could see my entire future. I would perfect my English, fill orders for the business more efficiently, and delegate the sales to my brothers. Plus, I would train like hell. I had no idea that Bill Lee didn't think much of my swimming. That he never considered me to be Olympic material or that he had a whole other plan in mind. All I knew was that I was exhausted. Not from training or running our business, but from the emotional toll of shouldering such a significant load for my family at such a young age. I'd become a middle-aged teenager and California sounded like freedom.

"Yes, Mr. Lee," I said, "yes!"

73

All that matters,

all that exists

in this life is the

present moment,

and the effort you

bring when the

pressure is on.

3

Strait of Gibraltar

Weary from 33 hours of travel, my eyes bloodshot, I trudged toward my hotel room in Tarifa, Spain at 2:00 a.m. on July 2nd, 2015, and found a note taped to the door. It was from Nora, and it was not good news. I read it twice, shook my head in resignation, entered my hotel room, pulled back the shades, and looked out across the Strait of Gibraltar toward twinkling lights on a far shore. Sometimes your only choice in life is to accept your fate.

I was the last of my team to arrive, which normally wouldn't make much difference because there's always lag time baked into the front end of a marathon swim. Typically, swimmers reserve a weather window of seven to ten days with their boat captain and arrive on location a week early to acclimate the body, get in the water and feel the conditions before that window opens. Even then, there's often a short wait (one night, maybe two or three) before conditions trend toward the ideal, the channel gods open their arms for a daring swimmer to test their resolve, and the captain gives their swimmer—because when it comes to weather and timing it is always the captain's call—the green light.

———

As a marathon swimmer, all you can ever do is accept the circumstances, adapt, and continue to give your best.

———

This time, things were different. According to the note, a storm was brewing. Heavy winds dominated the forecast for weeks, wiping away all the good weather days within the window I'd reserved and beyond. According to Nora's note, the only chance I had to swim was the very next day, and I was to meet my team on the docks for a 10:00 a.m. departure.

That's a quick turnaround. Unreasonable, really, but you cannot fight the weather. As a marathon swimmer, all you can ever do is accept the circumstances, adapt and continue to give your best. At least the channel gods, and our captain, Rafael Gutiérrez, gave me one chance. It would be up to me to seize it.

This time I would not swim alone. There were four Mexican swimmers in Tarifa that week and all of us planned to swim the channel, independently, over the next two weeks. Given the weather forecast, we were offered two options: swim together or not at all.

That meant Nora, my coach and crew chief, would be in the water too, along with our friend Mariel Hawley and her 16-year-old son, Eduardo Rodríguez. We called him Lalo. Like Nora and I, Mariel had already crossed the English Channel and circumnavigated Manhattan Island. Lalo was a new open water swimmer and he and Mariel were dedicating their swim to the passing of her late husband and his father, Eduardo Sr., who had died just three months before.

Mariel had always been an athlete. The granddaughter of an English war hero, she grew up hearing stories of how as a frightened soldier, her grandfather had shoved off from the English shore, and made his way to France to fight in the World War I. As his ship motored out of port, he looked back at the white cliffs of Dover and promised himself that he would see them again. Three years later, he returned to England victorious. Mariel loved that story and though she was a junior tennis player growing up, swimming had always been her favorite sport. But it wasn't until 2007, when she was 38 years old and part of a record-setting relay team that crossed the English Channel four times, that she would first see the Dover bluffs.

I met Mariel in 2009. We did the Manhattan Island swim on the same day, and soon after that she went to Dover to swim the English Channel solo, with Nora as her coach. She planned on having her father along with her, but he died of a stroke a few months earlier. She wound up swimming the English Channel in his honor, and to honor his father, as well, and finished in 14 hours and 33 minutes. When she crossed the Catalina Channel in 2012, she achieved the Triple Crown of Open Water Swimming.

Swimming the Strait of Gibraltar had been her husband's idea. He knew that she was happiest when she was training for a big event, and Eduardo was an avid traveler and loved the idea of taking the kids to Spain on vacation. Then his cancer diagnosis upended their lives.

Lalo refused to attend school. He wanted to spend all his time with his ailing father and his grades suffered. During one of the good periods, when it appeared that Eduardo was responding to treatment, Mariel suggested to Lalo that he swim Gibraltar with her the following summer. By then, he'd become a great swimmer too, and was excited about the possibility. So was Eduardo Sr., who was feeling well enough to travel. The catch was Lalo had to go back to school and keep his grades up.

Unfortunately, three months before the swim, not long after his final brain surgery, Eduardo died. By then, swimming a channel was the last thing on Mariel's mind and she thought it made better sense to sell her reservation. Lalo stopped her. He wanted to follow through with the swim and honor his father like Mariel had done in England. This wouldn't be just another channel swim for them, it would be a memorial pilgrimage.

When I first decided to take on the remaining five swims and complete the Oceans Seven, Nora had been my first phone call. Admittedly, my motivation was a bit vain: I was not yet considered a great open water swimmer by my peers. I'd completed the Triple Crown of Open Water Swimming and was the first to do all three in a calendar year (when I was 50 years old), yet for five straight years I was passed over by voters for the International Marathon Swimming Hall of Fame. The Oceans Seven was a relatively new concept in 2015, and my hope was that by completing it, I'd prove myself to anybody who still doubted me. Nora was a willing coach and after dedicating myself to running marathons and climbing mountains for the previous six years, she designed a program to get me back in swim shape.

I was in the pool five days a week and at Las Estacas for a long swim, once a week. These were difficult grinding pool workouts, better suited for younger swimmers—we're talking about 50 separate 100-meter sprints every 90 seconds or so—and because I had taken so many years off with very little swimming, my mechanics were out of sync. Although I wracked up 20 kilometers of swimming in the first week and ratcheted up my output from there, my arm angle was out of place and my left shoulder couldn't handle the mileage. It hurt like hell. I'd ice it after my pool workouts and sought electrical therapy to reduce inflammation in my shoulder joint. Nothing worked. I just swam through it, and tried to ignore the pain and my nagging self-doubt.

I cloaked my insecurity and told everyone I could that I was going after the Oceans Seven. I thought by making it known, I'd become driven to overcome any and all obstacles. Of course, I never mentioned I was nursing an injury that didn't seem to be getting better. If anything, as Gibraltar approached, my arm got worse. Even Nora had no clue that in the weeks before I arrived in Tarifa I'd stopped swimming much at all. I opted for rest, hoping my body would repair itself before I put it to another difficult test.

My nephew, Pablo, is a gifted photographer and he flew in to help crew my swim and to take pictures. He met me for breakfast at 8:00 a.m. on the day of the crossing, but I didn't eat much. Although it's tempting to pack on the calories before a long endurance event, I never overeat the morning of a marathon swim. I had coffee, some toast and fruit, which was enough.

At 10:00 a.m., Pablo and I met up with the others. Lalo was quiet and looked a little nervous. Mariel was concerned too. Her son had never swum more than eight kilometers at once, and this swim would likely be twice that. But it wasn't the distance that concerned her. It was his grief. She feared that failing to make it across would only compound his loss.

Nora was antsy. She'd arrived in Spain on a mission to break the all-time channel speed record and had expected to swim alone, and crew for me, Mariel, and Lalo on two separate swims. Now she had to be part coach, part athlete and I could sense her impatience before we even boarded our support boat.

Then there was my shoulder issue, and the fact that I never enjoyed swimming in large groups. The point is, from the beginning the energy was off. Nothing felt right, and yet there was the sea, lapping at the docks, glimmering in the morning sun, daring us to swim to Africa.

The Strait of Gibraltar is a slender waterway that stretches from Punta de Tarifa in Spain to Cires Point in Morocco, connecting two continents, millennia of history, and the Atlantic Ocean with the Mediterranean Sea. It's also one of the busiest shipping lanes in the world with over 300 merchant vessels crossing the course that the channel swimmers make daily. That's more than a dozen ships running across the course every hour. Each channel has their own hazard and those tankers, plus the wind, which funnels through and kicks up intense and unpredictable currents, make Gibraltar a difficult crossing, though it is the shortest channel of the Oceans Seven.

As a crow flies it's "only" 14.4 kilometers between Spain and Morocco, which still requires a major effort. But given the currents and swell, most swimmers end up covering between 16 to 20 kilometers when they attempt the strait. Although the water is rather deep, up to 900 meters in some places, its temperature is a mild 21°C. Hypothermia is rarely, if ever, an issue in Gibraltar. Nora and I figured we could make the crossing in under four hours, which is why I scheduled it first. It was part of a plan to build my stamina to tackle the longer, colder swims when my body and mind had been re-conditioned to the sea, and I was once again a hardcore open water swimmer, built to endure.

Mariel, Lalo, Nora and I dressed in Speedo swimsuits, caps and goggles—old habits die hard—and coated our skin in zinc to block out the sun. Then we loaded up in a Zodiac which would be escorted by a larger, 50-foot long fishing boat to make sure our small convoy of swimmers could be seen by the hulking tankers that plowed through the strait night and day. Our support crew included my nephew Pablo, Nora's half-brother Oswaldo, and Andrea, Mariel's 14-year old daughter, none of whom had any idea what they were doing. Luckily, another gifted Mexican swimmer, and seasoned coach and crew chief, Paty Kohlman, was still in Gibraltar. She'd coached one of her swimmers across the strait just a few days before. When Nora heard about our weather problems, she called Paty and asked her to be our crew chief.

Paty proved to be our angel. With no notice at all, and very little time, she dropped everything, went to the supermarket and bought all of our supplies—food and water—and worked with Nora on a plan that would see us across the channel. Or so we hoped.

At a little after 10:00 a.m., we shoved off from the Spanish coast. Our Zodiac buzzed along the sun-dappled shore of Tarifa proper. We marveled at the moldering remains of a medieval fort rising above the old city, the timeless malecón, and noticed a distinct Moroccan influence on the local architecture. Even more beautiful were the turquoise shallows that kissed pristine, white sand beaches on the rural edges of the city.

Fifteen minutes later, we idled off the jumble of rocks and boulders that form Punta de Tarifa. One by one, the four of us jumped into the water. We grouped up for a photo and a prayer on that rocky edge, then set off, determined to swim to Africa.

It was a warm day and a moderate wind rippled the surface as we swam in a tight group between the boats. Before we left, Nora and I agreed that she shouldn't try and break any records. "Let's swim at Lalo's pace," I said, "and make sure he makes it." She agreed, but Nora is a competitor and when she has a goal, it's difficult for her to let it go.

To my surprise, it was Lalo who pushed hard at the beginning of the swim, which meant one of two things. He was a stronger swimmer than I thought, and I should stop worrying about him and focus on my own swim, or he was riding the false high of adrenaline, and would soon hit a wall. Either way, all I could do was wait and try and keep pace myself. Easier said than done. I felt my shoulder twinge with every stroke.

In the meantime, Nora was busy monitoring my every move. When I swam close to her, she warned me not to draft. Drafting—or swimming in another's wake, which is easier than moving through undisturbed water—is against the rules in open water swimming and if the observer with the Strait of Gibraltar Swimming Association saw a violation, he might void the entire swim, disqualifying not just me, but the others as well. If that happened, we'd have to come back and do it all over again. But when I avoided the group and swam wide of the Zodiac, Nora shouted at me again. This time she wanted me to come closer, lest I be mowed down by some unobservant supertanker. I rolled my eyes but obeyed.

83

We kept to the same rituals I remembered from the English Channel, Manhattan Island and Catalina Channel crossings. We would drink something every thirty minutes, and eat at the top of the hour, but with four people to serve in the water and only two available crew members (Pablo and Oswaldo were on a different Zodiac taking pictures all day)—each with their own prioritized allegiance—our breaks took longer than usual. We were swimming 53 minutes for every hour in the water, and in a channel with unpredictable currents, we all knew that could become a problem.

Paty kept us laughing through the anxiety. She and I loved to tease one another. "You are really doing bad," she told me as she handed over my water bottle. "I really don't think you will make it." I knew she was kidding and loved teasing her right back, which picked up the spirits of the entire group. Recently, she told me that she was doing that because she assumed I was suffering from sleep deprivation and wanted to take my mind off it. She didn't realize that my shoulder was in bad shape, and that part of me wondered if I would, in fact, make it to Morocco.

Things got worse when Lalo cracked in the second hour and began lagging behind. We were forced to stop time and time again so he could catch up, which was frustrating, but I could only imagine what he was going through. What else could he be thinking of during the long crossing to Morocco, but his father and his broken heart? Mariel was crying most of the way too. She was thinking about Eduardo but was also worried for Lalo. She remembered how her success in the English Channel helped her cope with grief after her father died and desperately wanted that same solace for Lalo.

I felt for both—especially Lalo—but stopping so often threw us off course and keeping up a consistent pace is critical for long crossings. Nora set a slower but steady pace and she insisted we all follow her lead, but at our next break, Lalo was still suffering. Chafed and sun burnt, his shoulders tense and stiff, he sucked from his water bottle, tears in his eyes.

"I don't know if I can finish," he whispered to me.

"Listen," I said. "Just take it easy. We're halfway there already and we have all the time in the world to finish. If it takes us four hours, five or six, it doesn't matter. We just want to finish." He nodded and wiped his eyes.

While he refueled, I called to Nora. It was illegal for me to touch her at all, even just to tap her on the shoulder, so I motioned her away from the support boat.

"You and Mariel swim ahead," I said. "I'll stay with Lalo."

She was reluctant but agreed. It felt good to have some space and swim in our own patch of blue water. If nothing else, I hoped that even a modest adjustment like that could recalibrate and refresh Lalo's mind and allow him to tackle the swim without his mother's concern and his coach's instruction weighing too heavy on his soul. He couldn't stop his pain anymore than I could, and Morocco wasn't going to somehow magically float towards us. The only hope he had was to accept his suffering and use it to find something deep within himself. He had to become the open water swimmer that he promised his father he would be.

Whether he realized it or not, he had reached a pivotal point in his life. The pressure was on, his physical and emotional pain peaking. Would he quit or endure? Given my injury, I was in a similar position, but I had a lifetime of

85

accomplishments to draw from for strength and courage. He was a newbie and this swim—whether he succeeded or quit—could define his life for years to come. Mariel was aware of that possibility, which is why she'd been so concerned.

In the wake of his father's death, Lalo was learning yet again that in most cases, life will not happen the way you want. When you set a big goal, the path to achievement is rarely, if ever, easy or effortless, and when those difficult moments come and your world feels as though it's collapsing all around you—when you've lost someone you love, are fired from a job, dealing with divorce or financial troubles, moving away from home, or wrestling with any other brand of uncertainty, pain, or failure—it's tempting to think of what might have been or wish for an easier path.

We all do that. But you can't change the past, and the future—the one you've been hoping and dreaming of—doesn't exist either. It's an illusion. All that matters, all that exists in this life is the present moment, and the effort you bring when the pressure is on. But to stay present demands acceptance of what is. It requires flexibility and a willingness to adapt to the circumstances that surround you, no matter how displeasing or chaotic.

That's what I was doing with Lalo. Sore as my left shoulder was, I knew slowing down would help both of us. It felt good to alter our plans and try to adapt to what we were both going through. That act alone didn't relieve our suffering much, or promise Lalo and I successful crossings, but it gave our minds some control of what we were experiencing, it lightened our emotional load, and empowered us to persevere.

As I swam alongside Lalo, I allowed my mind to drift back to something my father taught me when I was a year younger than him, on the precipice of my own pilgrimage, my own life changing journey. We were sitting outside in the sun when my father looked over and said, "Do you know why the dinosaurs died?" I turned to him and blinked twice, unsure. "They were the biggest and strongest animals on Earth, but now they are all gone because no matter how powerful they were, they could not adapt to the changing conditions on Earth. They couldn't change when circumstances demanded it." He paused to let his lesson sink in. "Life is easier when you adapt, Toño. Never forget that."

Lalo's ongoing internal struggle and my worsening left shoulder aside, there was only one near-disaster in the Strait of Gibraltar. It happened in the third hour. By then we'd seen all manner of massive ships buzz by us. There were coal barges and military vessels, and several container ships too, but it was the car ferry that came closest to killing us.

For several terrifying minutes, it looked to be heading straight for us, but our escort boat was able to maneuver and act as a shield. We also slightly altered our course, to let the ferry churn ahead and leave us in its wake. The whole episode took twenty minutes, which allowed Lalo and I to catch up with Nora and Mariel, eat and drink. When we started swimming hard again, we were all refreshed and inspired by the Moroccan coastline that loomed closer with each stroke. Especially Lalo. He finished strongest of all.

When we got within 100 meters of the North African shore, Nora and I hung back as mother and son swam onto the rocky beach so they could share their moment of love, grief and accomplishment. They embraced and wept. After a few moments, Nora and I swam in to officially complete our crossing of the Strait of Gibraltar in four hours and twenty-three minutes. We embraced, then stood arm in arm, toes dry, all of us looking triumphant as the Captain blew his horn to salute our victory. Pablo's photos captured the moment, and if you look closely, you'll see all four of us grinning ear to ear. But my smile was a lie.

My aching shoulder was killing me.

We didn't linger in Morocco long. Our visa wouldn't permit it. Instead, we loaded up in the fishing boat and began the hour-long cruise back to Spain, where we feasted on tapas and paella, and sipped Spanish wine at a restaurant on the docks. I usually love celebrating channel swims with prolonged post-swim feasts, but for me that meal was bittersweet because I knew I wasn't merely sore. I was injured. Perhaps seriously.

For months I'd tried to ignore the truth, but given the distances of the channels still to come, I knew denying it any longer was pointless. Once again, I would have to adapt my training to include rehabilitation and possibly recalibrate my swim schedule altogether, but would that be enough? I was 56 years old, and way past my prime as an athlete. Sometimes older athletes break down and there is nothing they can do about it. Father Time, as they say, is undefeated. When I boarded a plane from Tarifa to meet Lucía in Madrid the next day, I should have felt satisfied. I was a step closer to achieving an audacious goal, but it had never seemed further away. My dream of completing the Oceans Seven was very much in doubt.

89

STRAIT OF GIBRALTAR

In the pool I

could forget

myself, tunnel into

complete focus on

the task at hand,

and feel a fleeting

sense of peace.

4

Adapt

Helen picked me up in her convertible at 8:00 p.m., as promised, and in minutes we'd turned onto a canyon road that wound through the Los Altos Hills. She pulled into the last remaining parking space on a dark street, 100 feet from the biggest house on a leafy block. We could see kids streaming into it from all sides. She turned to me and smiled.

"What kind of a party is this?" I asked.

"A keg party. I told you."

"I know, but… what's a keg?"

I smiled. She laughed and rolled her eyes at my naiveté, took the keys from the ignition and got out of the car.

In many ways I was beyond my years as a teenager. I owned and ran a business. I'd traveled internationally many times, and I spoke three languages, but in other ways I was sheltered and out of my depth. I was a 17-year-old kid who had never been to an unsupervised house party with other teenagers before.

"Come on, I'll show you," she said. "Tonight, you can teach me Spanish, and I will teach you about America. Or, you know, the Los Altos version or whatever."

I hesitated, still unsure. She lingered there in the muted streetlights, her wavy light brown hair catching the glow. Sensing my hesitance, she turned and began strolling toward the mayhem. I was sheltered and perhaps ignorant, sure, but I wasn't stupid. I shot out of the car and hurried after her.

We entered the garden through a back gate that was wide open and she pointed toward a mob of kids crowded around a trash can piled with ice.

"That's the keg!" She had to shout, because even though we were close enough for me to feel her breath on my cheek, the Rolling Stones were blasting from some nearby speaker, and there was so much laughter, shouting and singing, I could barely hear her. I followed her finger to the scrum and saw kids with big paper cups filling them to the brim with foamy beer. "Do you like beer?" She asked.

"I've never tried it," I said. She looked at me funny. Her eyebrows scrunched up when she grinned.

"Antonio," she said, "you're like a brand new baby." Then she kissed me on the cheek.

It was my first week in the US, and I barely knew Helen. We'd met at the pool. We were both members of the Los Altos High School swim team, and the fact that I was painfully shy in my new surroundings drew her in. She told me she was going to show me around, and to be ready at 8:00 p.m.

"Ready for what?" I asked.

"Your future," she said.

But as we inched closer to the keg, cups in hand, the spinning red and blue lights of local police cars flashed through the trees, and a handful of officers pushed into the garden from the open back gate. My pulse raced. In Mexico, the police behaved with relative impunity, but American cops scared me even more because I had no rights. I was a visiting student and if they arrested me for underage drinking, I could kiss my golden opportunity (i.e. my student visa) goodbye. Helen saw the terror in my eyes.

"I know a back way out," she said. "Come on."

She took my hand and guided me through an oak grove that rambled down a short slope towards a creek that led to the street nearby her car. We jumped in. She started the engine and without turning the lights on, flipped her car around and sped off. Once we were out of sight of the police, she flicked on her headlights and flashed that smile again.

"Fun party, huh?" She rolled her eyes. "It's okay," I know another one. More intimate."

Fifteen minutes later, we pulled up to an even bigger house in the hills, but this time there weren't dozens of other students cramming into the garden. When she opened the unlocked front door, I saw familiar faces, two teammates of ours from the Los Altos High School swim team, and one of the school's best divers, along with their girlfriends.

It was the diver's house. His father was an Admiral in the Navy, and the six of them were having beers in the kitchen. Helen waved hello, they nodded back, then she led me down a hall—the walls decked out with presidential photo ops and

93

framed medals—and out the back door to a deck with a Jacuzzi and a magnificent view of the Pacific Ocean.

"Let's get in," she whispered, gesturing toward the hot tub.

"I don't have a swim suit," I said.

"We can... skinny dip?" She set the notion afloat in the air like a casual question. Like it was no big deal. Fear and sex collided in my brain and coursed through my veins, as I looked over my shoulder to the kids in the kitchen, illuminated in the windows. Every bit of me wanted to undress with that beautiful girl, but her free spirit terrified me, and I was intimidated in my new surroundings. California was the kinetic energy buzzing all around me. It was the golden moon on my skin, the gentle warmth of a bright morning sun, but it was not yet in my blood.

"Maybe we can just sit here and enjoy the view," I said. She sighed and sat down.

"Of course we can," she said. But a few minutes later, when our conversation died down, she got up, went inside the house to socialize, and left me on the deck, alone.

Helen never did become my girlfriend. I didn't have time to date. I arrived in Los Altos with a two-year plan. I would study, swim and, if all went well, by the end of the second year, I'd qualify for the Mexican national team and compete at the Central American Games. That put all my focus on swimming and studying.

I settled into Bill and Shirley Lee's home as a middle-aged teenager. On the weekends, I'd sit and read the business section with Bill at the breakfast table, and at school I was treated as the oddity that I was. Exchange students weren't common in those pre-globalized days and there was a distance between me and the other kids that was hard to bridge. The teachers seemed more interested in me and where I came from than my classmates, and most days I ate my lunch alone. I rarely went out at night and if I did, it was always with the Lee kids, Debbie and David. I was the designated driver because I refused to drink. I was forever in training.

Though I was a bit of a loner, I got my crash course in Americana. I was shocked when they handed out our text books for free on the first day of school. In Mexico, text books are only free in primary school. In high school we have to pay for them. I'd also never been to an American football game and hadn't seen cheerleaders either. So, my first Friday night football game set my head spinning. I loved the camaraderie and the school spirit. Lettermen jackets were a new phenomenon for me too, and I knew I'd earn one of my own. In fact, from the beginning I was the second-best swimmer in school, and its 200-yard and 500-yard freestyle specialist. My only friend, Monty Brown, was our Michael Phelps. He wasn't just the best swimmer in our school. Monty was one of the best in the entire Bay Area, which was saying something.

I'm not sure there is a more competitive environment for junior swimming anywhere in the world than the San Francisco Bay Area's. Club meets far surpass high school competitions when it comes to contentious rivalries and overall competitiveness. Parents and swimmers decorate their cars days before meets. Bleachers are always packed, crowds are rowdy and the talent in the pool does not disappoint. I knew that from my very first practice with the De Anza Swim Club.

The leap from my original YMCA pool to the Olympic Pool in Mexico was a puddle jump compared to the transcontinental performance gap between the Social Security team and De Anza. Our coach, Bill Rose, was internationally renowned, which meant for once I was surrounded by real talent and would be nurtured by top-shelf coaching. The best swimmer on the team was an 18-year-old named Mike Saphir, who had barely missed making the 1976 Olympics by a tenth of a second. Monty was our second best and then there was everybody else.

In the glittering 50-meter outdoor pool at De Anza Community College, there were no slow lanes. All of them were stocked with great swimmers, boys and girls. Mike led the first lane, Monty led the second lane and I led lane three. But the lanes were co-ed. A handful of girls swam in Mike and Monty's lanes and were better than I was. I was in the upper middle of a pack of about 100 swimmers, and nearly all of them would one day compete at the college level.

During that first workout, I was torn between two emotions: fear and awe. Right away, I knew I'd made the right decision in moving to California, while at the same time, I realized it would require an even higher level of effort and commitment than I could have predicted. The quality of swimmers in just the first four lanes at De Anza was so high that almost all of them could easily qualify for Mexico's national team. While intimidating, it also inspired me because if I could just hang with them, it would prove that I could get there too.

I was the only Mexican in the swim club, but it wasn't my heritage that made me feel separate from the team. It was my life experience. I'd always put the U.S. on a pedestal, mostly because of my relationship with Bill. But once again, I was seeing I had more in common with the adults around the team than my teammates, whose perspective on Mexico was rather narrow. Several were shocked when they found out I'd, gasp, tried doughnuts and hamburgers before. They weren't well read. To them, I was this exotic creature from another planet, but, to be frank, kind of boring. To me, they were the boring ones. Or maybe I was just homesick. Luckily, Monty was shy and nerdy like me, so at least I had one ally.

My schedule wasn't much different in the States than it had been in Mexico. I woke up at 4:30 a.m. most mornings to get in 10,000 yards of swimming before school started (in the U.S. swim races are measured in yards instead of meters). Then I'd attend classes and swim again in the afternoon. During my first summer in California, I was at De Anza College seven days a week, spending at least six hours in the pool, swimming 20,000 yards daily. Coach had us doing 100 100-yard sprints before he'd even say hello. We'd finish each sprint in just over a minute and usually have five to ten seconds to rest before we took off again. The pace was brutal, but I was soon in the best cardiovascular shape of my life. Even though I never medaled in club swim meets, my times were getting better, good enough to make the Mexican national team.

On the surface, everything was lining up as I'd hoped. I made real strides in the pool, Bill and Shirley treated me like their son, school was easy, and Bill took great pride in my grades, but I didn't enjoy my first year in California because I felt so alone. In hindsight, there were three issues eating away at my well being.

First, I over trained. 20,000 yards of swimming each day is a lot for anybody, especially a teenager. Sports science wasn't robust in those days. Back then, coaches thought the only way to build peak performance was to increase yardage and pace. Now that kind of thinking is viewed as prehistoric. The point is, I was exhausted and never took a break to catch my breath and let my body and mind recover. Second, some of the coaches at De Anza couldn't help but comment on my weight. I was never a skinny kid. I always carried a little bit of weight around my middle, and my coaches' comments, and the snickering they invited from my teammates, made me feel even more self conscious. And when you take that level of exhaustion and real insecurity and blend it with schoolwork and being immersed in an entirely new culture, you can see how I might have felt like a flabby fish out of water whenever I was actually out of the water.

It didn't help that Bill Lee loved to eat at great restaurants. In those days, San Francisco was second to only New York in terms of an abundance of ridiculously good American kitchens. Most of the time he brought me along, taught me what to look for and how to order. Shirley was a great cook too, so even when we stayed home for dinner, there was always a feast. But with my self esteem suffering and my coaches berating me for my weight, I lost perspective.

One evening, I ate so much after a long workout, my belly felt like it was about to explode. I ran into the bathroom, took off my shirt and stared myself down in the mirror. My belly looked more bloated than ever. It disgusted me. I disgusted me. I felt so bad, mentally and physically, that I jammed my finger down my throat and made myself vomit. The relief was instantaneous. Vomiting came with an endorphin flush that made everything feel so much better, but there was some guilt too. I knew what I'd done wasn't healthy, so I told myself it was a one-time thing, something I'd never let happen again.

But then it did happen again, and again after that. Soon I was throwing up at least once a day, and sometimes twice, for most of my senior year in high school, while I was still putting out all that energy in the pool. My bulimia was a brainworm I couldn't shake. The first time I did it, my action was a response to physical discomfort, but within days I had trouble discerning if the physical discomfort I felt was real or imagined. Which meant than anytime my belly was full I headed for the bathroom to empty it out. I became slimmer, sure, but I was also in the grip of a dangerous eating disorder. One that can kill, and like most of us that have suffered in this way, I kept it a secret.

I'd taken a step back from my swim goods business. I still organized shipments for my brothers—Raúl was running the business back home—but for the most part, I stayed out of it. All I had was the water, my studies, my dark secret, and my solitude. Most of the time I was in turmoil. Sometimes I felt like ending it all. Suicide crossed my mind more than once. Yet even on those awful days, in the pool I could forget myself, tunnel into complete focus on the task at hand, and feel a fleeting sense of peace.

In February 1978, during my second swim season in California, my goal was to break 4:20 in the 400m freestyle and 16:45 in the 1500m freestyle. Those were the benchmarks I'd have to hit in order to qualify for the Mexican national team the following April. Despite my bulimia, my times

99

had improved steadily and at the Central Coast Section Championships, I finally broke through the five-minute barrier in the 500-yard freestyle, which meant I was closer to achieving my 400m goal. I didn't win a medal but rising out of the water and seeing my time post had me feeling like I'd won the Mexico City championship all over again.

A few weeks later, at the Santa Clara Invitational, I fell seven seconds short in the 1500m, but seven seconds isn't much in a 30-lap race. I was right where I needed to be and that gave me confidence when I traveled to Veracruz a month later to compete at the national team trials in advance of the Central American Games.

My father and grandfather traveled with me to Veracruz where I was one of the favorites to make the team. Everyone knew where I had been living and training. I was the guy who had risen out of Mexico's stunted swim scene, found some real coaching, and at nearly 19-years-old, was ready to claim his rightful place on the national team. Except that's not what happened. I didn't have any energy that day. I wasn't nervous, just empty. Bulimia had caught up with me. I didn't have a second gear and could never find the rhythm I needed to keep up with the leaders. I labored and flailed, and ultimately failed. It was humiliating.

Given my precarious mental health and illness, you might have thought such a defeat would drive me deeper into depression. Instead, my failure dissipated the dark cloud that had tracked me for so many months. When I returned to Mexico City, I went to the doctor for a blood test. He would ultimately find that my zinc levels were dangerously low, which is common for anorexics and bulimics. That was a loud wake up call. A few days later, I called Bill Lee and broke the news that, despite his generosity and connections, I'd failed.

He listened but didn't seem too bothered about it. He'd always kept tabs on my times, but whenever swimming came up, I got the sense that he saw my destiny in a more complete way than I could at that age. He never saw me as an athlete alone and swimming, it turned out, was not the main reason he'd invited me to California.

"Well, you know what they say, Antonio," he said, "When one door closes, another one usually opens."

"What do you mean, Mr. Lee?" I still called him Mr. Lee. Many years passed until I felt comfortable calling him Bill.

"You got a packet in the mail today." I could practically hear his smile beaming through the telephone. "It's from Stanford University."

Bill Lee was a Stanford alumnus, a financial booster of the university all his adult life, and I hadn't even told him I was applying to his alma mater, so I knew he was surprised. My application to Stanford was filed like the way most of us file prayers with God. It was a pipe dream. Although my grades at Los Altos were excellent, I got 950 out of 1600 on the SAT. That's a terrible score, but my perfect score on the Test of English as a Foreign Language (TOEFL) and glowing recommendations from teachers made up for it.

When I arrived back in California, Bill invited me into his study to discuss my options. I'd been accepted to several schools, but Columbia was the only school to guarantee me a spot on the swim team.

"I know you love swimming, Antonio, but Columbia isn't a swim power, and those coaches won't turn you into a top

Olympic swimmer. Plus, you'll be freezing in the winter. Why not stay close to us," he said, pulling his chair just an inch closer to deliver the second biggest surprise of my young life. "I've already called coach Jim Gaughran. He's got a spot on the Stanford swim team waiting for you."

If you handpicked all the best athletes I ever swam with or against in my life and put them all on one team, the Stanford swim team would still be in another stratosphere. I was swimming with some of the best of the very best. The men's team standouts included Mike Bruner, the 200m butterfly gold medalist at the Montreal Olympics in 1976. He'd made headlines when he shaved his head with a straight razor prior to swimming in the finals. Nowadays, that kind of thing is not uncommon, but it was a radical move in 1976. Paul Hartloff was another teammate. He was a towering, lanky figure who set an Olympic record in Montreal in the 1500m freestyle.

I wasn't fast enough to hang in the men's lane so I landed in the women's lane, which was no picnic either. Jo Harshbarger Clark was the best of the women. She held the world record in the 1500m freestyle. Valerie Lee held the American record in the 200m butterfly. Then there was Kim Peyton, an Olympic gold medalist in the 4x100m women's relay in 1976. Jo was petite, sleek and fast. Kim was over six feet tall and the prototypical athlete. Valerie was as strong as they come, yet I did manage to keep pace with them in our distance workouts when each morning and afternoon we swam 800m intervals at top speed.

But I was not on a swim scholarship, which meant money was tight. With all my attention focused on my studies, our swim business was in a lull, and some days I was so hungry I was forced to show up at the Lee house just in time for dinner, or I'd meet Bill in the city at one of his favorite restaurants. I was no longer bulimic, and it was a comfort knowing I had family to lean on.

I loved Stanford right away. There was the rambling, wooded campus, studded with century-old stone buildings, plenty of pretty college girls with bright open minds, and in my first week at Stanford, I made a friend for life.

Brad Howe and I met on the second day of classes. Wearing long curly hair, a Mongolian sheepskin vest, and clogs—I embraced my inner hippie during my freshman year—I shuffled into a small lecture hall early one morning. Punctuality has always been important to me, but to my surprise I wasn't the first to arrive. With so many empty seats, I thought it would be weird and maybe even rude to sit in some far-off corner of the room, so in that empty room, I sat right behind him, which made him laugh.

After class, we got to talking and went to the Lagunita dining hall for breakfast. At Stanford, the first question any freshman asks any other freshman is about their SAT scores. Most students got near-perfect scores and every time I heard a 1400 or a 1500, I felt pangs of pride in having one of the worst SAT results in the entire university. I asked Brad about his as we grabbed plates and joined a line along a ribbed counter where we could peruse steaming stainless steel trays of a chunky substance that looked like scrambled eggs, congealed, overcooked strips of bacon, cold sausage, limp hash browns and so much more. We loaded our plates with all of the above.

"940," he said.

"Bullshit!"

"Hand to God. You?"

"950."

"That's a great score," he said with a laugh.

"I thought I was going to be the dumb one," I said.

"Sorry. That position is filled," he said with his right hand over his heart. "I guess we know why we wound up in 8:00 a.m. freshman calculus," he said.

We laughed as we made our way through the checkout line to a nearby table. "You want to hear something really funny?" He asked. "I'm on scholarship."

"You're an athlete? Which sport?" He shook his head.

"Academic scholarship."

"With those SAT scores?" I asked. "What kind of corrupt university is this?"

"You know, when I got in, I thought it was some kind of mistake too. Then I figured out what happened."

"And?"

"I got lucky."

Oh, yes, I liked Brad right away. Luck wasn't his story though. Like me, he got into Stanford because of his grades. From an early age, he latched onto doing well in school as a way to stay sane. He was born into one of the most dysfunctional families you could possibly imagine, and his studies allowed him to withdraw, tune out the chaos, and eventually offered a way out, but he didn't share any of that with me right away. That first morning, he mostly just listened.

He thought I was from the Middle East and was surprised when I told him I was from Mexico. I shared my passion for swimming and he mentioned that he was a surfer, but we didn't bond over the water because I wasn't an ocean swimmer yet. Instead, we discussed Latin American economics and politics, and my newfound passion for Marxism. Brad had spent a semester in Brazil during his senior year in high school and confessed his love for Latin America. He tried to speak some Spanish, but I was forced to confess that his Spanish was horrible.

As an avowed Marxist, and new student at a highly competitive university, I still had a reduced relationship with my swim goods business, and my brothers weren't doing much with it either. So, I joined the proletariat and took a job scrubbing dishes in the cafeteria. I soon found that line of work was not for me and the money wasn't nearly enough to cover my books, meals and everything else. I badly needed a cash infusion.

The mandatory introductory course for all students majoring in economics at Stanford back then was Econ 1, taught by Michael Boskin. It was held in a vast lecture hall crammed with 500 students. Early in the year, I met another freshman named Andrea. We became friends, and after missing class one day she asked me for my notes so she could study and catch up. When I handed them to her, she was shocked.

"Wow. Your notes are very good," she said. "We could sell these. Students would pay good money for them."

Just like that, another business was born. Andrea typed up my notes from class on her portable Olivetti typewriter that night and edited them. When midterms and finals came, she ran copies on a mimeograph machine and we sold them on White Plaza. One day, my roommate James Isaac saw us together. James had attended Choate Rosemary Hall, an elite prep school on the East Coast, and knew Andrea. When I got home, he made sure to educate me as to who she really was.

"You know who Andrea is, right?" He asked. "Her last name, I mean?

"Yes, Mellon."

"Exactly."

"What are you trying to say?" I asked, totally clueless. James laughed.

"You know… Andrew Mellon, the famous banker?"

James went on to wonder aloud why Andrea Mellon would feel the need to hustle for money when she was obviously a rich girl, but I understood. Even in my Marxist period, that's one thing I loved about Stanford. The children of some of the most powerful parents were hustlers like me. I washed dishes alongside the son of a Senator and another kid whose father was the number two executive at American Express. So what if Andrea loved the hustle and wanted to make a bit of money on her own terms? I thought that was pretty cool. From then on, I sold my notes from every economics class I took.

On the whole, my life was very good, except when it came to my main thing: swimming. In late October, I was lapped at a Pac-10 meet (today the conference is called the Pac-12). We were competing against UCLA, another powerhouse, and I was swimming the 1650-yard freestyle, the longest individual race in any meet. It happened toward the end of the race. It was the first time I'd ever been lapped in any swim meet going back to the YMCA, and it was both humiliating and heartbreaking. Heartbreaking because it was the most definitive proof yet that I would never become an Olympic athlete and humiliating because all of my Stanford teammates had been there to bear witness. Yet, despite that, I was not cut from the team. Because our coach, Jim Gaughran, was good friends with Bill. I'd known him for some time, and he'd always liked me.

In fact, the following Monday I was back at practice, swimming my 800-yard intervals as usual, but my heart wasn't in it and my pace was a half-stroke slow. Typically, I led lane three, the one with all the accomplished women. They liked swimming behind me because I opened up the water for them, but that day, my pace annoyed them.

Jo kept slapping my feet while Kim and Valerie shouted at me to go faster. I offered to swim behind the three of them, but they weren't interested in that. It seemed that as far as they were concerned, my role on the team was to provide assistance to the top athletes, which makes sense now that I think about it. Playing a supporting role on a championship caliber team is a privilege, but I didn't see it that way at the time. Instead, not yet halfway through the afternoon's workout, I climbed out of the pool and walked over to our coach.

"Jim," I said, "I'm over this. Thank you very much for the opportunity." Jim Gaughran was a great coach. He had won a national title at Stanford, and he knew I didn't belong in that pool, but he was such a gentleman that he never would have cut me. So I did his job for him. I just shook his hand and walked away. Away from the dreams I'd cultivated as a child and from a sport I loved more than anything in the world. From that day forward, I swore that swimming would no longer define me. In fact, I wouldn't slip into another lap pool for nearly 20 years.

Brad and I settled into a routine that first year in school. We were both painfully competitive and we usually studied together deep into the night. The only break we allowed for ourselves was a nightly dispatch to the on-campus coffee house for a slice of the best carrot cake ever divined by God or man, and an hour of backgammon.

One day he suggested that we make a road trip to Southern California to visit his family during spring break. We stopped for a night in Santa Barbara and then spent a second night at his stepfather's house in Hollywood Hills where we lounged on the deck and stared at a sea of glittering lights spread across the LA basin.

"Where's your mother? Is she here?" I asked.

"No. She doesn't live here. Not anymore," Brad said.

"She's been married and divorced twice then."

"Well…" I turned to face him.

"How many times?"

"Six maybe? Could be seven. I haven't counted lately."

"Don't bullshit me, Brad. Seven times?"

"Actually… it's eight… now that I think about it." I took a long look at my new friend, who was torn between the obvious humor of a ridiculous revelation, and the memory of the deep and real painful consequences on his upbringing. I thought about where I'd be without such a strong mother and knew it wouldn't be Stanford University or the Hollywood Hills.

The next day we drove south to Laguna Beach where he attended high school and met up with his surfer friends, including Greg French. Greg lived with his parents in a magnificent house overlooking the beach. He'd go on to become an artist. We also hung out with his friend, Marvin Freeman, a stylish bohemian kid with a variety of quirky sunglasses. Marvin would eventually launch the Oliver Peoples brand of glass frames. The sun shined down on Laguna Beach all day every day, the girls were beautiful, and I enjoyed piecing together Brad's backstory.

Brad told me that he moved every year or two and though he'd lived in a handful of spectacular homes, none of them belonged to his mother anymore. She was broke. Finally, after four days we went to see his dad at his place in Hemet, a small rural town in the desert mountains of Riverside County. Hemet was another of Brad's many hometowns.

Brad's father worked out of a house that always seemed to be under repair, and as soon as we arrived, he told us that if we wanted to stay a few nights, we were going to have to work for it. He pointed toward a pile of paint cans and put us to work painting the house. In the evenings we would take Mr. Howe's motorcycle out for a ride on the wide-open country roads, as the sun settled behind the scrubby mountains and the air cooled just enough to keep us sane. Velocity rippled my cheeks and fat mosquitos smashed the lenses of my sunglasses as I accelerated beyond 130 km/h. It was pure exhilaration.

The following summer, after freshmen year wrapped up and we'd all moved out of our dorm rooms, I brought Brad with me to Mexico. After what I'd seen, I knew that there was a void in Brad's heart and soul and that there was only one way to fill it. He needed a family. Upon his arrival, my mother made sure to note Brad's favorite foods and drinks and stocked up. My father offered recommended reading. Brad fell for our ferocious (at first) but generally friendly German shepherd, and my brothers adored him.

I introduced Brad to our neighborhood *organillero* and the *zócalo* life of Coyoacán. Around ten, we would leave the house without any idea where the day would take us. We'd just walk and explore. Our youngest brother, Arturo, was five years old by then and constantly tagging along with us. If we weren't careful, we would leave the house without closing the gate behind us, stroll down the street 100 meters or so, and when one of us looked back, he'd be there. Which meant we had to take care of him for the rest of the day. He was as persistent as he was precocious and with three older brothers, and now Brad, Arturo was guaranteed to grow up fast.

Growing up with so many different addresses, ever changing role models and life circumstances to contend with, Brad felt like an outsider, anywhere and everywhere he went. That's one of the reasons he thought it was a mistake when Stanford accepted him, but living with us that summer in Coyoacán he found a sense of belonging. After just one week, both my parents approached Brad separately and told him that they considered him their son too.

In 1980, the summer when Brad and I were in Mexico City, Chile was wrapped in a cloak of unapologetic fascism. A CIA-led coup had toppled the would-be socialist government and Augusto Pinochet took power in 1973 with an eye toward silencing his critics one way or another. Intellectuals, journalists, artists and musicians went into exile by the truckload, and many came to Mexico. I was tapped into that underground and each night there were parties in the basement *peña* bars all over Coyoacán. Brad loved to party in those rooms filled with South American folk music, poetry, and revolution. Musicians jammed on the guitar, charango, pan flutes and drums. They read Pablo Neruda and testified to the right-wing crackdown that saw friends and family beaten, killed or taken as political prisoners. There was laughter and heart ache, and a feeling of deep solidarity.

Yet for all my lefty leanings, the truth was that once we arrived back in Palo Alto on the eve of our sophomore year, I was weary of being broke and sick of washing dishes. Spending the summer with my brothers in Mexico made me realize that without my leading the charge, our swim goods concern would shrivel and die. I needed to delve back into business in a significant way, so I called Nelson in Mexico, went to see Bill Lee, and made sure my brothers Diego and Raúl were ready for the re-launch. This time, I told them, we would become bigger than ever.

At first, I ordered the out-of-season stock, the stuff that didn't sell, from Speedo's factories in the U.S. and Canada, and purchased everything at a price below wholesale. Then, Diego, Raúl, and Eugenio Castañeda—Diego's friend from school whom we ended up loving like a brother—would drive from Mexico City to Guadalajara, making stops in Querétaro, León, and Guanajuato to identify the sporting good stores. They set up appointments with the owners, showed them our stock and began taking orders for swim caps, goggles, and swimsuits. We were no longer simply serving kiosks and swim meets in Mexico City. We expanded and were looking to stock the entire country.

In order to handle the bigger demand, we applied for import permits. By then Mexico was beginning to open up little by little, but the permissions process was convoluted and took months. Sometimes it took years. That's how inefficient Mexico was in the early 1980's. Yet we persevered, eventually received our permits, and kept growing locally. But we were hungry for more.

Although I was just 22 years old, I'd made a good number of contacts through Bill Lee. Since I had always followed through on all my promises with him and spoke good English, I was able to convince every American producer of swimming equipment—caps, suits and goggles, lane lines, kick boards, face cloths, pull buoys, and even starting blocks—to let us represent them in all of Latin America. Licensing was a relatively new business back then. Nowadays, that type of privilege would cost large sums of cash. We got the rights for free, mostly because Bill Lee wrote letters of introduction, and when the company sales people called him to sound me out, he told them, "Trust Antonio. He will deliver."

That's how we closed the deal on supplying the World Cup swim meet held in Ecuador, in 1981. I arrived at the new swim stadium in Guayaquil while it was under construction (they were still digging holes for the pools) and approached the World Cup organizers. I introduced myself and gave them a list of all the items they would need for their meet. The boss, who was in his forties, dismissed me rather quickly.

"Why would I order from a kid?" he said, "I plan to go straight to the manufacturers."

"Okay," I replied, "You do that. That's a good idea."

I left without applying any pressure because I knew there would be nothing they could buy that we didn't control. When my phone rang two weeks later, I was very nice, took his order, and let him know the price and when he could expect delivery. By the end of the call the World Cup organizers and I were laughing openly about how a few smart-ass kids from Mexico City could pull something like that off.

By the time my junior year began I was driving a new red BMW sedan. Brad took one look, nodded and said, "I guess you're not a Marxist anymore."

"Capitalists drive nicer cars," I said.

After Guayaquil, we began supplying pools and competitions all over Latin America. We even handled the Pan American Games in Venezuela. These were the days before ATM cards, and blink-and-you'll-miss-it cash transfers. We had so much money coming through so many different accounts that I sometimes wound up paper rich, but cash poor.

In 1982, I remember visiting Brad in Rio, where he was enjoying a semester abroad. While he opted for a long overland trip through South and Central America, and Mexico, before returning home, I caught a plane to Venezuela to pick up a check. The problem was I didn't have a Venezuelan visa, so when my plane landed, the Pan American Games committee sent the check by courier and it was delivered to me in the customs office in the Caracas airport. Eventually, I was deported to Isla Margarita, but since I was out of cash and there was no bank that would cash my check, I slept in the airport until my flight to Miami the following morning.

Business was so good, Raúl started taking flying lessons, and when the Formula 1 series put on their first race in Los Angeles, all of us were there. All except little Arturo, of course. Raúl, Diego, Eugenio, and I booked a suite at the Beverly Hilton, and the day before the race we rented a plane at the Van Nuys airport and made Raúl fly us over the Formula 1 racecourse, and along the coast in Malibu.

Our race day seats were ideal. We sat among celebrities and industrialists, and had the time of our lives. Looking back, I can see how things might have gone horribly wrong, but none of us drank much back then. I still hadn't even tried beer yet. Wine and liquor were not a part of my world either, and nobody in our group took drugs. We were four straight-laced capitalist kids making it rain.

In fact, the first time I tasted beer, I was a senior at Stanford. It was in 1982, just after I'd met a young economics professor from Mexico City named Jaime Serra. 1982 was a difficult year in Mexico. A devaluation of the peso had torched the economy. Inflation skyrocketed. There were shortages in shops across the country. Many families lost their life savings, and he was at Stanford teaching a course on why and how it all happened. His was a vital, new, technocratic economic retrospective, but his class had a rather bland academic name: Recent Economic Developments in Mexico.

All I knew about him before we met on the first day of class was that he was Mexican. I didn't know he'd been educated at Yale and had been considered a big-time professor at El Colegio de México. In fact, when I saw him outside the building before class, he looked slightly disheveled and lost, so I approached him.

"Do you need some help?" I asked. He nodded and handed over his syllabus.

"I need to get this photocopied." In Mexico, he'd had staff who waited on him hand and foot. At Stanford, he was a solo act without so much as a graduate assistant and he wasn't handling it too well. After class I properly introduced myself, and within days I was his assistant, his fixer, his indispensable staff of one.

Three weeks into the semester I learned that Jaime was a runner. Jogging was becoming popular in the United States, and he invited me to join him. I'd been running ever since I quit the swim team and was quite good, but I let him stay in front, out of respect. It was a hot day, and after running ten kilometers through the Stanford campus, he invited me into his apartment and shoved an icy beer in my hand. He knew I didn't drink and found it ridiculous. I watched him take a satisfying swig, then stared at the bottle in my fist. Suds bubbled up and snaked down the neck onto my finger tips.

"Drink," he said.

I took a sip, licked my lips and smiled. Then I took another. Jaime nodded, pleased with himself. A great friendship was born.

"Whether you

do it or don't

do it, for me

you will always

be my hero. So,

go and enjoy

your swim!"

The Tsugaru Strait

I tried not to dwell on my pain on the flight to Tokyo, but it was hard because I knew this trip, this swim, was going to make or break my Oceans Seven dream. With only a handful of training days left, it was clear that once I hit the water and attempted to swim between the islands of Honshu and Hokkaido in northern Japan, one of three things would happen. I would either find a way to adjust my stroke to eliminate the pain that I was experiencing in my left shoulder (doubtful), grit my teeth and suffer for the full crossing (if that was even possible), or the pain would prove too much, I'd quit, and then be forced to reevaluate the probability of ever achieving the Oceans Seven (my gravest suspicion).

Yes, the Tsugaru Strait would be a crucial test. Not just because of my physical condition, which hadn't improved since I surfaced in Morocco at the end of the Gibraltar swim, but also because the water in northern Japan is cooler than the Mediterranean, the weather more unpredictable, and the distance a lot longer. Gibraltar wasn't a significant physical challenge by marathon swim standards. Tsugaru would be.

There were also logistical headaches. Japanese law wouldn't permit me, or any licensed Mexican driver, to rent a car if we didn't also have a European or American license, so I had to organize some other form of transport. Not just for me, but for my entire team, which once again included Nora and Pablo. Then there was the cultural element. We were heading for Cape Tappi on Honshu Island, Japan's largest landmass where Tokyo, Kyoto and Osaka are all located, though our destination was far less electric. Tappi is a tiny fishing village on Honshu's blustery northern cape, and we weren't sure if there would be adequate food or any nearby shops to stock up on supplies for the crossing.

Thankfully, one of my business partners linked me up with the head of Mexico's tourist board in Japan, Guillermo Eguiarte. When I called him to share my transportation concerns, he assured me it wouldn't be a problem. That's all I needed to hear. I figured he'd arrange a driver and a translator to meet us at the Narita International Airport because I knew the odds of finding Spanish speakers on Japanese soil were about the same as my learning how to speak Japanese on an overnight flight. It wasn't going to happen. But when we arrived and gathered in baggage claim, we weren't met by a Japanese driver in a dark suit, holding a sign written in Spanish or English. We were met by Guillermo himself. He'd heard my story by then and wanted to be there to witness my attempt. He also wanted to contribute to our team in some way and decided that *he* would become our driver and translator.

Guillermo and his wife, Lolita, picked us up at Narita Airport and drove us across town to Haneda Airport, a smaller, domestic airfield where we boarded a short flight to Aomori. That's where Guillermo rented a car and drove us on a succession of narrower and narrower roads into the Japanese countryside. 90 minutes later, we arrived at Cape Tappi, the northernmost point on Honshu Island. There was only one major hotel in town, the Tappizaki Onsen Hotel, set mere steps from the bluffs.

It was late at night by the time we staggered from the car toward the lobby doors, and as we crossed the parking area, we saw one of the hotel's staff emerge from a back door to take out the trash. He looked a young 30-year-old, was dressed in kitchen whites, and when he heard us speaking Spanish he glanced over as he dropped the garbage in the dumpster. He wiped his hands on his apron and approached us just as we were about to enter the hotel.

He bowed and welcomed us to Tappi. Not in Japanese or even English. This man spoke Spanish. None of us could believe it, not even Guillermo. His name was Tetsuo, and he told us he once lived in Mexico for a year, studied Spanish there, and still loved the language. It was obvious he was very excited to see us and explained that he had never heard Spanish spoken in Tappi. He didn't linger for long, but his warmth and his language skills were a great omen for the hospitality to come.

Still, after 28 hours of travel from Mexico City, what we all really needed at that moment was some rest. The hotel rooms had sliding rice paper dividers between a sitting area and the bedroom, where we each had a choice between a normal mattress or a tatami, a thin mat made from woven straw, rolled onto an elevated platform that was strewn with pillows. I stared out the window at the moonlight glinting off the distant sea and decided to try falling asleep the traditional Japanese way. I slept like a baby.

The next morning, we met downstairs at 7:00 a.m. for breakfast, as planned. The dining room was packed with Japanese tourists, with the exception of two tables: ours and another group of three in the far corner. They were people who I knew from the open water community: American swimmer Dan Curtis, his Irish friend, and their Italian coach Valerio Valli.

Although the northern coast of Honshu Island is very beautiful, with its leafy, craggy bluffs and secluded bays where locals harvest seaweed and fish in the surf, the weather isn't always so serene. It can be overcast, windswept and cold, and the village is more of a working marina, home to deep water commercial fishing operations and squid trawlers, rather than a haven for foreign tourists. In fact, the majority of international travelers who stop in Tappi for any length of time are marathon swimmers eager to test themselves in the Tsugaru Strait.

But just because someone wanders the world to swim across oceans does not necessarily make them a good traveler. It should, because a large part of what makes someone a great open water swimmer comes down to how well they can adapt to adverse conditions and maintain poise and power. Adaptation is also a critical component of any good traveler.

To get the most out of an adventure on foreign soil requires a desire to maintain an open heart and mind, embrace local customs, and enjoy the local food. Your hosts will be able to feel that and open themselves more to you.

Athletes, though, can be a controlling bunch. Some of us tend to zero in on what we need above all else, especially when it comes to our fuel and time to train, and when those needs aren't met, it's easy to become agitated and fail to adapt to the circumstances that surround us. And failures we don't understand or see coming, even meaningless ones, often lead to subsequent, more substantial failures.

The swimmers I knew had expected a big western breakfast. They'd completed a crossing the night before and wanted to refuel with a heaping portion of sausage, eggs and toast. But that isn't a Japanese breakfast. At least not in Tappi. Breakfast in our hotel was fish and rice.

This isn't usually a problem for their primary clientele, Japanese train geeks who arrive daily by bullet train and stay overnight to gather and watch locomotives disappear into a tunnel that plunges beneath the Tsugaru Strait. That's the main draw to Tappi. For breakfast, the hotel chef would simply cook whichever pieces of sashimi that weren't eaten at dinner and serve them. We never knew which fish we'd be served. Yet instead of embracing the mystery of local custom (and the superiority of Japanese cuisine), the swimmers complained. The wait staff bowed in apology and promised to have what they desired the following day.

Watching that minor drama play out brought to mind something my mental coach, Jaime Delgado, mentioned when I first set out to achieve the Oceans Seven. At the time my training was sluggish. It took longer than I hoped to find my form and it was frustrating.

"You're looking at all the little things and focusing on little problems all the time can be dangerous," he warned. "It's as if you're in a room and you light a match. The match itself, that small flame, is nothing to worry about, but if you drop the match onto the carpet, it may catch on fire, and if you still don't notice or do anything about the fire, it's going to spread to the drapes, and destroy the entire room. And after the room, it's going to swallow the whole house. So, you have to be able to get around those little things, those negative thoughts, because if you don't do that, your house—which is your goal, your entire objective—is going to turn to ash.

"What you are trying to achieve is so difficult," he had said, "You must respect that. And the best way to do that is to maintain a positive mindset for the challenges you know lie ahead."

As the swim party got up to leave, I leaned toward Nora and Pablo. "The three of us, our team," I said. "We will embrace Japanese culture. That means eating the food and trying everything once."

"And being respectful and grateful," Pablo added with a smile.

"Exactly," Nora said. "It is such a privilege to even be here."

From that moment on, our collective mindset of openness and gratitude not only helped us find joy in the day to day, it helped me face the fact that I had a very long swim ahead, and only one sound shoulder to get me all the way to Hokkaido.

We'd arrived in Japan on September 5th, 2015 and settled into an early rhythm. After breakfast, we'd rest for an hour or two and then go for a swim. Landing on location early can cause problems for some swimmers, but I wanted to give myself every opportunity to adjust to Japanese time.

Nora wasn't enthusiastic about my swimming long distances before the crossing. She wanted me to taper, so my body would repair all muscle damage and I could maximize my strength at the perfect time, but I had to feel the water. I needed to know what I was up against.

At first, we found a beach near the hotel, strewn with sharp volcanic rocks, where the water was deep blue and crystal clear. After a few awkward steps, it was easy to relax and enjoy the sea.

Those mild one-to-two-hour swims allowed me to experiment and find an arm slot that would propel me, for as long as necessary, with less pain. I was looking for my forever stroke. I wasn't going to heal overnight, and to make it across the Tsugaru Strait I needed to find the place where it hurt a little less.

Nora swam alongside and watched me carefully. Sometimes I felt a twinge of pain right away, other times it wouldn't appear until after about 15 minutes of swimming. Whenever it happened, it was up to me to adapt and adjust, and the only adjustment I could make was to shorten my stroke, which made me a much slower swimmer. That worried me because I wasn't all that fast to begin with and because Tsugaru is known for its strong currents. The odds were that in order to be successful, at some point I would have to lengthen my stroke and go all out.

At first it was just Nora and me in the water, but soon an Indian swimmer named Rohan More joined us in Japan and all three of us swam together. We became an object of curiosity in town. A seaweed collector who watched us train on her beach began bringing down jugs of warm water for us to rinse with after emerging from the sea, which was welcome because the water—which was about 18-19°C— was a bit chilly. Later in the week, she invited us for a tea ceremony in her lovely home on the cliffs.

When it came to his nutrition, Rohan and his family also had issues with the hotel dining room. Like the others, they craved the familiar, but they didn't have a car and there was no fleet of taxis in Tappi waiting to ferry guests to the nearest grocery store, an hour away. So, on their second day in town, Guillermo drove Rohan and his mother—the team chef—to stock up on ingredients for vegetarian Indian dishes. I tagged along.

It was no secret that Rohan was pursuing the Oceans Seven too, and his most recent success was the North Channel. The North Channel wasn't the longest swim we'd face, but thanks to its low temperatures, and its reputation for fierce jellyfish blooms, it intimidated me, and most marathon swimmers, more than any other. Rohan was 33. He was a top athlete in peak condition, but when he showed me pictures of himself staggering from the water in Scotland after completing the channel, I was shocked. He had brown skin, but in those photos his color had been vaporized. He looked like a shivering ghost; like death itself. My ass froze just looking at him.

But I had more immediate concerns. Before sunset that evening, I walked up a hill in search of a panoramic view to take in the Tsugaru Strait. In Japanese, Tsugaru means "the mouth of the wind," and the wind that night was so strong that I had trouble standing still. The waves in the channel were enormous. Boat traffic came to a halt. My shoulder throbbed while my mind swirled with uncertainty.

Rohan arrived in Japan after me but was scheduled to swim on September 13th. Though he completed the channel (his fifth of the Oceans Seven) in ten hours and 37 minutes, his swim didn't exactly make me feel any better about my own chances. Nine hours into it, he had hit a current, where the Pacific Ocean and the Sea of Japan merge, that pulled him backward. To overcome and continue to push forward to the northern shore, he had to dig deep and swim with all his power. And he had two good shoulders, was over twenty years younger and a lot faster than me.

For ten days, I'd countered my anxiety by enjoying Japanese life. The food was fantastic. During our long lunches and dinners, Guillermo regaled us with stories of Japanese art, architecture and photography, or Japanese jazz and classical music. He's one of the most well-read people I've ever met, and he turned every meal into a symposium, but not a boring one. I enjoyed sleeping on the tatami and taking Japanese mineral baths, steamed to the ideal temperature, first thing in the morning and again after my training swims. In the afternoons, I wrote my blog. Those habits helped me keep things simple, but whenever the swim itself popped into my mind, the pain in my shoulder burned, and stress foamed to the surface of my mind.

On September 15th, the eve of Mexico's Independence Day, my time arrived. Our team woke up at 3:00 a.m. and waited to be picked up by our boat captain and his crew, who were late, and as the clock ticked my pulse thumped faster and louder. I felt the pressure. My gut and mind swirled with unease.

At 3:20 am, my phone pinged with a text message. It wasn't the boat captain. It was from my daughter, Ximena, who had arrived in Japan the day before, and was waiting for us in Tokyo. It was as if she was reading my mind in real time.

I know you're not feeling well and have a lot of doubts whether you're going to finish it. But whether you do it or don't do it, for me you will always be my hero! So, go and enjoy your swim!

Her message brought me to tears. Ximena and I never discussed my swims in advance. She always knew my plans and tried to meet me wherever I swam, but we didn't discuss my health or the hazards that I was prepared to face because I knew they made her nervous. I hadn't even told her about my shoulder. Yet she was tuned into how I was feeling.

They say when we love someone, we can sometimes feel their pain, struggle, and joy, from hundreds, even thousands of kilometers away. Her message proved that and instantly lifted the pressure off my shoulders. From that moment, my primary objective was to enjoy the swim, and from there, figure out how to get it done.

At around 4:00 a.m., we boarded our chartered fishing boat, the 11-meter long *Dai-Shichi Koei Maru* (Japanese for Number Seven Honor). While we motored from the marina to our starting point, ten kilometers south of Tappi, my team smeared zinc on my skin to protect me from the sun and also taped up my shoulder for added support. I'd been looking for any and every possible solution to my shoulder problems and my doctor, Ariadna, suggested KT tape— the athletic tape used by elite athletes all over the world to ease swelling and pain. Nora had been concerned that other swimmers and the channel swimming association might consider it an illegal advantage and protest my results, but two days before, Steven Munatones, the head of the World Open Water Swimming Association, allowed it and the Tsugaru Channel Swimming Association followed suit. Not that the tape did any good.

In the moments before a swim begins, it's easy to drown in self-doubt. With 30 cold-water kilometers ahead—at its narrowest point, the strait is 19.5 kilometers wide—it would be unreasonable to be free of all insecurity. The ocean is too strong a force and we humans are so meek by comparison. But it's funny. Once you finally jump in from the end of the boat, reach your starting position and start swimming, most of that anticipatory stress melts away. All there is is the simple act of swimming and the beauty of the sea.

At 4:00 a.m. on September 15th, 2015, with our boat idling off the very tip of Honshu Island, I jumped in and swam to my starting position. The first thing I noticed was that the water had warmed up to 20°C, comfortable enough for a long swim. The wind was calm, the sky clear, and though my shoulder hurt right away, the pain felt manageable in the early stages. Plus, I was pleased because another potential problem I'd anticipated had been solved by the captain.

During most channel swims, we swim parallel to our support boat. Usually, when I swim, the boat motors along my right side, the side I prefer to breathe, and if there is a kayaker in the water they stay on my right, as well. In Gibraltar we didn't have paddlers, but the Zodiac was in perfect position, along our right side the whole time. That positioning makes the boat easy to follow. I don't have to think about my course because I can see the boat with every breath. In the run up to the Tsugaru swim, when I was taking inventory of all the variables I'd have to manage to be successful, I marked the boat position as a concern. I was worried that the captain would position his boat on my left side, which would make it much harder for me to follow and find my flow.

But Captain Mizushima set my mind at ease immediately by unfurling a line called a swim streamer with a flag trailing from the very end. It was weighted to hover in perfect position, just in front and below me, so I could follow it as if I was in an infinite pool following a lane line. With Ximena's message burned into memory, and this easy-to-chase carrot, I felt a wave of relief wash over me, and I locked into an early rhythm that felt like a moving meditation. I could feel the ocean flow and froth around my skin as I cut smoothly through it. I was able to find an arm slot and shortened stroke which mitigated most of my pain, and with the wind still light, and the rising sun spreading a pink dawn over the waters of northern Japan, I racked up the kilometers.

That's not to say it was easy. As soon as I moved out of the shadow of the cape, beyond the sheltering influence of Honshu Island, and into the open channel, I could feel the swell build. By mid-morning, I was rising and falling with a swell that was nearly two meters high. Since I couldn't extend my arm fully, there were times I couldn't lift it high enough to break the surface. But once again I found a way to adapt and keep moving. I swiveled my hips to roll over on my right side more completely in order to break the surface with each and every stroke. Most importantly, I just kept swimming.

My entire team wore specially designed shirts and sweat suits I had made for the crossing. They were silk screened with the names of the three channels that I'd made so far—English Channel, Catalina and Gibraltar—with a box checked alongside them, and at the bottom was Tsugaru Strait, with its box still unchecked. Every time I stopped for a feed, I could see the work I still had left to do. The truth was motivating. It kept me humble and focused.

My nutrition was the same on this swim as it always is. Whenever I stopped, Nora approached me with a bottle of water mixed with Accel Gel and a white board, which held a message. Early on, her messages were about my pace or the complicated current. Tsugaru's shifting tides are always a puzzle to solve, and they are the main reason it's considered one of the more difficult crossings in the world. So, it didn't surprise us that on September 15th, 2015, the currents kept switching direction and we were forced to change course more than once.

What got me through was limiting my thinking. I had a team of people on the boat whose job it was to chart my course. I couldn't worry about what I could not control so I left it to them and wiped it from my mind. My sole job was to keep moving, count my strokes, and follow the flag. And by doing that, I was able to enjoy the journey just as Ximena had suggested, even with the maddening tides and the severe swells, which produced another drama worth monitoring: our dear Guillermo's bout of unrelenting sea sickness.

Oh, poor Guillermo. He knew so much about so many things, but a sailor he was not. When he said he wanted to join us on the boat for my swim, I agreed immediately, but from the moment he set foot on deck, he was uncomfortable. Soon enough his face flushed a queasy green, but he was trapped. Both of us faced a full day of suffering. I just hoped and prayed that as he puked his guts out, I'd be spared his backwash. Thankfully, in that regard, the channel gods answered my prayers, but when it came to my heart's true desire, they did not go easy on me.

For most of the day, whenever I swam up to the boat to refuel I could see the Hokkaido shore loom closer and closer. Progress was palpable and that drove me forward, but in hour ten I hit a steel curtain current and no matter how hard I swam, I didn't move a single inch for nearly two hours. It was a surreal feeling. I could see the shore, floating just three kilometers away, but I couldn't make any progress.

During one break, as I sipped my water and energy gel, I must have looked slightly discouraged. Nora saw that and wrote Tsugaru on her white board with an empty box next to it, waiting for my check mark of success. She didn't say anything. She just stared into my eyes. I nodded and got back to work.

Within a few minutes, I was finally able to move. It was barely noticeable. Perhaps a few centimeters for every tenth stroke, but it became gradually easier from there, until, at last, I broke through. As I swam closer to shore, land began to pacify the open water. The swell and the wind calmed, and the surface smoothed until I was cutting glass again. From there it was just a matter of time.

Twelve hours and thirty-eight minutes after I jumped into the sea before dawn, I was able to feel sand and stones beneath my feet. With my crew watching and cheering from the distance, I took my time standing up. My legs wobbled, so I stood still for a moment before taking ten short, slow steps out of the tides and onto the rocky beach. With my toes dry, I stood beneath a classic Japanese archway and raised my bent arms. The captain sounded his horn.

My left shoulder throbbed relentlessly, and my equilibrium was still off, having bobbed in the sea for so long, but my smile was wide. When I first arrived in Japan, I had no clue if I would physically be able to make it the full 30 kilometers, and I'd done it on the eve of Mexican Independence Day, which made it even sweeter.

We motored into the Tappi marina at around 6:00 p.m., but before joining my team for a celebratory dinner in the hotel dining room, I hiked up to that panoramic viewpoint, so I could stare back out at the Tsugaru Strait. It looked as beautiful and as formidable as ever. I smiled, sat down cross-legged, and closed my eyes. Tetsuo saw me there from below and scrambled up the slope to join me.

"You looked like you were shining," he said. "You've done a great thing. Let's pray and give thanks."

He sat beside me and closed his eyes. I don't know how long we were up there meditating. Maybe twenty minutes, perhaps more. All I remember is a feeling of deep satisfaction saturating my mind and settling into my bones.

The following day my team and I flew to Tokyo and collected Lucía and Ximena. The day after that, Guillermo drove us outside the city to the Kamakura Temple, the Vatican for Shintoists, where we met Mr. Yoshida, the Guji (high priest) of the Tsurugaoka Hachimangu Sanctuary—one of the three most important Shinto sanctuaries in all of Japan. He told me that followers of the Shinto faith have a great respect for all who complete the Tsugaru crossing. In my honor, he performed a Kagura ritual, asking the gods for good fortune, channeling the forces of nature in a way that would allow me to fulfill my objectives.

As we stood at his altar, the scent of cedar wood washed over us, and I felt a calm yet vital buzz of energy. After he finished, Mr. Yoshida opened his eyes, turned toward me and asked me to make a wish. I stared into my hands and thought about how I felt physically, and about the challenges—those three more difficult swims—that lay ahead. Each would be its own riddle to be solved, its own rite of passage, and I already knew which one was up next.

"I want to finish Molokai," I said.

While the priest considered my wish, and paused to meditate on the answer, my mind drifted to the Ka'iwi Channel—a stretch of water between the islands of Molokai and Oahu in Hawaii. At 45 kilometers, it is the longest of the channel swims in the Oceans Seven.

"Well," the priest warned, "it's not a certainty. You must be well prepared. You must know that making the attempt alone is a great privilege."

I heard his words, but I didn't absorb them because I'd never felt the tumultuous fury of Hawaiian waters and I was still riding my post-swim high. All I knew was that the water off Molokai would be warm, and I was sure that if I could handle Tsugaru, the Ka'iwi Channel would be relatively easy.

The following summer I'd think of that moment repeatedly. I'd remember the tea Mr. Yoshida served alongside sublime tempura and though I've never been a spiritual man, as I swam and suffered in the water between Molokai and Oahu, I'd wonder just how much the Guji had known about my nightmare to come.

133

Between the Sea and the Ocean: Thoughts in Ink on the Waves of the Tsugaru Strait

The entire night churns the waves, the wind rages,
and the pines drip moisture, moonlight.

Matsuo Basho

We arrived at Cape Tappi, located at the northern end of Honshu, Japan's main island, in very high spirits, to witness one of the world's most complex crossings. Immediately, the sudden changes of climate, landscape, lights, and shadows that take place in this area of Japan inspired me to create a notebook of drawings that portray the setting of this great experience.

The peculiar geographical location of Cape Tappi makes it a melting pot, where the forces and warm currents of the Pacific blend with the cold waters of the Sea of Japan. As a result of this contrast, on the Pacific coast we find islets and rock formations where Japanese cedars have defied inclement weather for centuries. Challenging, they stand perched on the stones of these islets. On the other hand, the cold waters of the Sea of Japan have patiently carved out large cliffs and steep rock walls over time.

During the days before the crossing, while Toño caressed the waves and absorbed the *genius loci* of the Tsugaru Strait, in order to empathize with the ancestral forces that have always ruled it, I made a series of ink sketches of this magical natural scenery, alternating the waters of the Sea of Japan with those of the Pacific Ocean. Throughout these days of preparation, we faced strong winds, stormy showers, and frequent rains, but occasionally the sun came out. I took advantage of these sunny moments to try to capture the greatness and shifting magnificence of the landscape that characterizes Cape Tappi and the Tsugaru Strait.

135

GUILLERMO EGUIARTE BENDÍMEZ

Brief comment on experiences and sketches
made at Cape Tappi, Tsugaru Strait

August 14th, 2019

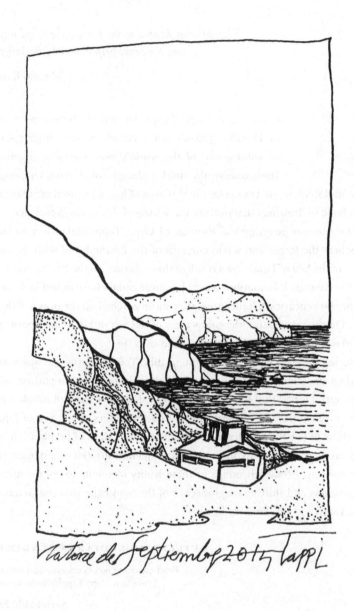

CHAPTER FIVE

Doce de Septiembre 2014 Tappi Aomori

Trece de Septiembre 2014 Tappi

THE TSUGARU STRAIT

It was time to shake off

the last vestiges

of the closed economy

that had dominated

Mexico for generations.

We were due for a

software update.

6

Going Home

In August 1982, Mexico's breaking financial news was revealed to everyone the way unsuspecting storms are revealed by Mother Nature: with pure devastation. For the second time in six months, bank accounts and equity were wiped out with the stroke of President José López Portillo's pen, which devalued the peso by another 30%. The combined effect of the two devaluations reduced the peso's value by nearly 50% against the dollar. Mexicans were suddenly half as wealthy as they used to be.

The move was made, according to the López Portillo administration, in the hopes of insulating the country from a coming recession. The theory was that Mexico's peso had become strong because it was propped up by the government, and that a strong peso hindered foreign investment on Mexican soil, while encouraging imports like, say, Speedo caps and goggles. Mexico had a large trade deficit at the time, which meant that our government didn't have enough foreign currency reserves to serve the debt it was carrying. The devaluations were proposed as a way to stimulate foreign investment, which would double as a solution to Mexico's credit problems.

Some businesses benefited in the short term, especially the real estate and tourism markets. Those who relied on imports were wiped out almost overnight. As I prepared to graduate from Stanford with majors in German Studies and Economics, our swim goods business was on the verge of bankruptcy. Then, in the midst of it all, my father landed in the hospital. He contracted spinal meningitis, and as a result had come down with cerebral edema, meaning his brain stem was swelling with fluid it couldn't drain. He needed emergency brain surgery to save his life.

My brother, Raúl, called to give me the news and within hours, I was on a plane to Mexico City, and my father was under the scalpel. I went directly to the hospital from the airport. The front desk directed me to the third floor ICU, and as the elevator doors opened everything felt like it was moving in slow motion. Doctors, nurses and attendants gathered at their stations only to scatter in all directions. I maneuvered around barely conscious patients on gurneys, and their shell-shocked loved ones who shuffled down the hallway in dread and disbelief.

At the end of the hall, Diego and Raúl sat in a small seating area tucked up against the wall. Raúl nodded and Diego gestured toward a doorway. I peeked inside and saw my mother holding my father's hand. He was intubated and unconscious. She wept and kissed his fingers. She didn't see or hear me. Over her shoulder, I could see an oxygen mask over my dad's nose and mouth, and IVs strung from a nearby rack draining fluids into his veins.

I took a step back and sat between Diego and Raúl. Nobody said anything for a while. I closed my eyes and flashed back to primary school when I used to do rounds with my father. He seemed such a towering presence then. He commanded respect. He knew so much about so many things, but when his career stumbled and he lost his job, he let that setback destroy him. If it weren't for my mother, his clinic would have collapsed too, and when he saw her propping the whole family up, he became lazier and lazier. He turned out to be weaker than I could have ever imagined.

I could have forgiven him for his weakness. I should have, but that would have required a level of empathy I wasn't able to summon as a 23-year-old. Instead, as I slumped into that chair, I hoped he would do us all a favor and let go. I wanted him to fade to black, once and for all, rather than become even more of a burden.

My mother was busy enough as it was, and my brothers and I had our own problems. The Mexican devaluation didn't just impact the domestic economy. The effects rippled through all of Latin America and it felt like everyone we were doing business with went belly up overnight. The people who owed us money couldn't pay us and we were facing a stack of invoices from Speedo, Keefer McNeil, our lane line manufacturer, and Duraflex, the company that made our springboards. We also owed money to Mondo, which manufactured rubber decking around the pools we serviced, and rubber grips for springboards and diving platforms. Our debt was huge.

Raúl, still just a 20-year-old industrial engineering student at the National Autonomous University of Mexico (UNAM), was running the day-to-day operations at the time, and he had a plan to get us out of the mess we were in.

"We have to declare bankruptcy," he whispered, breaking the silence. I looked over and shook my head.

"We aren't doing that."

"Toño, we have no choice. We have no income. Zero. It's over."

"If the business dies, it dies, but it's not over until we pay our bills," I said. "Only then will we consider closing the business or starting over."

"You don't understand how it is," Raúl said.

"Our manufacturers are in business too," I said. "They are people, just like us, with their own bills."

"You don't live here," Raúl said.

"And every single one of them had faith in me!" I raised my voice.

"Go to the shops. Look around!" Raúl was getting agitated too. Diego sat in silence taking it all in.

"Going bankrupt is easy, Raúl. Super easy. I'm going to honor my word."

"There is no more money, Toño. Where will find the cash to honor your precious word?"

I stood up. There was nothing more to say. I walked back down the hall, into an open elevator, and once on the ground floor, out the hospital doors. Anxious and frustrated, I stomped down the street, stopping in front of a small *tienda de abarrotes,* where you could usually find necessities like milk and butter, basic produce, snacks, and drinks. It wasn't a supermarket, but even in small stores, the shelves were usually full to bursting in Mexico.

Not that day.

After graduation I went home hoping to land a lead role in my family's and my country's revival.

I spent the rest of the afternoon wandering in and out of shops and supermarkets, one after another. I wish I had pictures because the images wouldn't be much different than what we have witnessed in Venezuela after 2017. With imports hampered, we were stuck with domestic brands, but with pesos now worth half as much, it was hard for shop owners to stay liquid enough to resupply domestically. Banks imposed withdrawal limits. The government set a hard ceiling on currency exchanges. Raúl was right. It did look like we, and the rest of the country, were in deep trouble, but I also knew there had to be a way out of the mess. All we needed was a little time.

My father didn't die, but he did spend a month in the hospital and never worked full-time again. Meanwhile, I returned to California to deal with the wreckage of our business and finish school. I called all our suppliers and gave them the news straight. I didn't sugarcoat the truth because I knew it wouldn't help. I told them we would pay them in full, but that it would take time, and every single one of them gave us time because we'd always paid our bills in the past. What I didn't share was that I had no idea how we would ever be able to come up with the money to pay them.

The weeks and months ticked by with our business stuck on life support. I had just one quarter to go in my fifth year at Stanford, and as finals approached, I fielded offers to work on Wall Street, and briefly thought about punting my obligations and escaping to film school at Columbia University. I'd applied earlier in the year and was accepted, but I couldn't bring myself to do it. I needed to work and start paying our debt, so after graduation I went home hoping to land a lead role in my family's and my country's revival.

Of course, I wasn't joining in the effort from a particularly powerful position. Gone was the BMW, the big contracts and the Pan American travel schedule. But it just so happened that not long after I returned home, Jaime Serra, my professor and mentor, decided to combine academia with public service and joined Mexico's government as an advisor to the Minister of Finance.

Serra was part of a new generation of Mexican leaders, a faction within the PRI, called the technocrats. They envisioned a smaller government, less tariffs and craved free trade partnerships with the United States and elsewhere. I was aligned with all those ideas, but Serra could only arrange an entry-level job for me at the Ministry of Finance. Beggars can't be choosers. It wouldn't solve my financial problems, but it was a start.

My early days in the Mexican government revealed how inefficient and mismanaged many agencies were. On my first day at the Ministry of Finance, I showed up for work at 7:45 a.m. because my office hours were supposed to be from 8:00 a.m. to 3:00 p.m. and I wanted to be early. I punched the clock and waited for my colleagues to show up. Most didn't trickle in until 10:00 a.m., when the office manager introduced himself and led me to a desk in the middle of a blank 15-meter-long corridor with nobody else in sight. That's where my career in public service began, moored on an island in the middle of a dry riverbed in a desert.

My boss, Ángel Gurría, was the Director of Public Credit at the Ministry of Finance. He'd agreed to take me on as a favor to Serra but didn't have time to deal with me. Instead, he suggested that I meet with five of his deputy directors and try to find some way to make myself useful, except they didn't want to provide me with an opportunity to show my value. They hoped to neutralize me by giving me almost nothing to do. For weeks, my sole job was to read the morning papers and clip the important news for the deputy directors. It's not that these men weren't working at all. They managed loans from multi-national banks in the U.S., Europe and Asia, the World Bank and other development and ex-im (export-import) banks, but they didn't want me in the room with them when they negotiated those deals.

It was a frustrating time, because without anything substantial to sink my teeth into, I couldn't prove myself and my future in government remained cloudy. Meanwhile my family's debt wasn't going anywhere and my salary, while good for a starting position in Mexico in 1984, didn't help much. I heard how much my Stanford classmates were making on Wall Street and couldn't help but wonder whether I'd made a grave error in coming home.

Early on, one of Gurría's personal assistants confided in me. "They are taking bets on how long you'll last," she said.

"Really... and?"

"Most are betting you won't last six months."

I did, and once our deputy directors realized I wasn't going to quit, they started giving me more to do. Little by little, I found file folders on the corner of my desk; loans with ex-im banks in need of renegotiation. By then I'd been in contact with my own creditors enough to have learned how to speak about money and debt in ways that impart confidence rather than anxiety. In other words, I was a proven negotiator and my success handling loans with Japanese, French and American bankers helped expand my responsibilities.

I was also one of the few people in the Ministry of Finance that actually enjoyed socializing with foreign bankers and diplomats. For instance, one of the deputies I reported to hated going out for Japanese food because he was a germ-a-phobe. He didn't like chopsticks or sharing platters or, worse, shabu shabu steam pots, so whenever those lunch invitations arrived, they would send me.

In 1986, Serra was appointed to be the Undersecretary of Finance, which placed him in command of the Mexican IRS, and I became his chief of staff. Our first move was to implement a Value Added Tax, which helped increase government revenues. With cash flowing again in Mexico, Raúl graduated from university with a plan to pay our debts in full and protect us from future devaluations. We pooled all of our money and managed to open a factory in Cuernavaca where we could manufacture caps, goggles, lane lines, and other swim goods, and continue to sell them domestically. We did continue to import Speedo swimsuits, however. After all, for Speedo, there is no substitute.

With business back up and running we were able to slowly pay off our debts and when we re-connected with Speedo to do business, our new connection, Carl Thomas, told me about an up and coming sport called triathlon. I was a very good runner in those days. I'd run a sub-three-hour marathon in New York and just over three hours in Boston, but I missed swimming, and the more I heard about triathlon, the more I saw it as a way to get back in the water. Trouble was, I worked a day job with the government, and lacked the time and money to fly off and compete in the States. Carl suggested a solution.

"Why don't you use your company to promote the sport in Mexico?"

Around that same time, Miguel Casillas, a close friend of Raúl's, asked him if we wanted to partner with him on a triathlon series. I loved the idea, so we met with Miguel and the Álvarez brothers—Antonio and David—and started a new company called MAAD Sports (now Asdeporte). We also formed the Mexican Triathlon Federation, and to this day Antonio remains a major force in the sport of triathlon internationally. We didn't launch the first triathlons in Mexico, but when we got involved, all the races held there had been amateur productions. They were one offs, and didn't have corporate sponsorship from big brands. We changed that by using Speedo's involvement to bring other international brands on board. So now I had three jobs—the swim goods business, triathlons, and my government position—plus I planned to compete in the races we organized, which meant I had to train, as well.

That was the fun part. Ever since I was in elementary school I'd been waking up at 4 a.m. to swim and I kept at it to train for marathons. Now, I needed to get comfortable on a bicycle because I'd never ridden a racing bike before. It was an easy transition. I had a friend pace me in the car before dawn each morning, and at that hour the streets were dead. Sometimes, we'd drive to the southern outskirts of the city where cars were forbidden, other times I rode the old highway, up a steep hill toward Cuautla where cacti grew on the roadside for kilometers. On the weekends we'd gather at a stadium where they held car races and ride the oval track.

I was living in a small apartment in the south end of Mexico City with my then wife, Mónica. And my bike—built from the best components and a top of the line, carbon fiber frame—cost more than all of our furniture combined.

"If Mónica finds out how much that bike cost," one of my friends liked to joke, "she will kill you."

"Be careful what you tell her," I replied. "She'd probably have us all killed."

One of the first things I noticed when I started riding was something I'd also become aware of when I took up running. Swimming set me up very well for success in endurance sports as an adult because when teenagers train in a pool by swimming interval sprints for hours at a time, they develop a lung capacity and baseline VO2 max that stays with them. Although my competitive swim career ended without an Olympic berth, it made me an athlete for life.

Mónica's family owned El Cid, one of the top hotels in Mazatlán, so that's where we held one of our first races. We arranged for permits to close the streets, but the police didn't do the job for us. We had to block off the streets early in the morning by ourselves. We set up the transition areas and met the athletes at the sign-in station. Raúl didn't enjoy competing, but I wasn't going to miss out. We also had a star in the field, a little-known teenage triathlete from Texas by the name of Lance Armstrong.

We did our best to present the event as professionally as possible, but we were a small, rag tag group of volunteers, and didn't have the technology to record split times. What we did have was a single running clock and some cans of paint. Whenever an athlete finished the swim our volunteers swabbed their arms with green paint. They got hit with yellow at the halfway point of the bike and red at the turn around point of the run. That way when they finished the run, we knew they'd completed all events in their entirety.

Looking back, triathlons gave me my very first taste of open water swimming, but I admit that I was not bit by the open water bug right away. Our races were Olympic distance, which was a 1.5km swim, followed by a 40km bike ride, and a 10km run. I was one of the faster swimmers, and one of the better all-around athletes in a field of about 100-150 competitors, but I was no match for the 16-year-old from Austin. Nobody was.

As soon as Lance Armstrong broke the tape, Raúl was there to shake the champion's hand, but Lance didn't greet him with a smile. He demanded his money right then. Raúl tried to explain that there would be an awards ceremony and he'd receive his check soon enough, but Lance wasn't willing to wait. In his defense, the 1980's were the wild west of triathlons. Races advertised large purses for the winners, but the money wasn't always paid in full, or even at all. The only things Lance knew about our race when he signed up, was that we were a new operation, he would win, and he wasn't leaving Mexico without his money. But he had nothing to fear. The Argüelles brothers always pay their debts.

Things were good in the 1980's. I got married, triathlons rekindled my passion for sports, and work was going very well, but I still hadn't figured out how to use my role in government to make an impact in Mexico in a way that felt personal to me. I was still searching.

The answers came with the election of Carlos Salinas as president of Mexico in 1988. Like Serra, Salinas was a technocrat with an eye on deregulation and the opening of Mexico's economy. Jaime Serra, who was being hailed as one of the country's finest economists, was the man he chose to get it done. Salinas appointed him to be Minister of Trade, and I became his Undersecretary of Administration.

The Salinas administration privatized long held government-controlled industries—most famously telecommunications—and abolished price controls. Until then, Mexico still didn't enjoy a truly free market. The government dictated prices and availability of brands in nearly every segment of the economy. Prices for soft drinks, tortillas, milk, and even marmalade were given hard ceilings. Most brands had maybe one or two competitors. Serra and I couldn't do much about that right away, but it was on our radar. Early on, however, Serra grappled with more pressing business, and I was assigned to more basic duty.

Although the North American Free Trade Agreement was ratified under Clinton, it was the first George Bush administration that launched NAFTA negotiations in 1989. That was Serra's chief focus, but it wasn't mine. While he worked on a glamour project, the first assignment that Serra gave me was to make sure all the bathrooms at the Ministry of Trade were sparkling clean. When he broke the news, he could see my confusion straight away.

"It's the best sign of a sound ministry," Serra explained. "You know if the bathrooms are clean, that everything else must be well-managed too. On the other hand, if the bathrooms are a mess, well..."

It was an interesting theory and it stuck with me because it was impossible not to notice how horrible most public restrooms were in Mexico. It wasn't that public toilets in the U.S. were always a slice of heaven, but the standard of cleanliness there tended to be higher, and I never liked what that said about my country.

I embraced the assignment and the first thing I did was hire bathroom attendants to stay in each bathroom at all times. We stocked them with enough paper towels and toilet paper so that we would never run out, and if someone stole our toilet paper—which did happen—we replaced it within minutes.

That first month we heard more than a few complaints. Most were concerned that we were wasting money, but we stuck with our plan and soon had the cleanest restrooms in the entire Salinas administration. After that, I upgraded our computer systems and made sure our technology was the best available.

The process reminded me of how I felt when I first sold Speedo and other swim gear, previously only available abroad, to people in Mexico. Upgrading our offices, and inspiring a higher level of maintenance, enabled me to offer my country something more, and it expanded the horizons—and the possibilities—of those who never had the opportunity to leave Mexico. That became my template for how I would focus my efforts in government for the rest of my career.

In 1989, Serra and Salinas hosted an economic summit in Puerto Vallarta. Twenty-five ministers of trade came from all over the world to determine trading tiers for the global economy. I was in charge of housing them, catering the meetings and organizing all the events. My biggest concern was to make sure that all the ministers stayed in the exact same class of hotel room. These men considered themselves on par with prime ministers (even though they weren't), and I didn't want any of them feeling they were being treated as favorites or, worse, being treated poorly by Mexico. Thankfully the Camino Real in Puerto Vallarta had just opened a new four-star tower in which every room was exactly the same. That's where I hosted all the ministers.

Most were friendly and warm, as politicians usually are (or pretend to be), but the Finance Minister of Japan was, well, kind of an asshole. When I met him at the hotel on the day all the ministers arrived, he treated me like a nuisance. First, he ignored me and when I extended my hand to introduce myself and pass him my business card, he handed me his golf clubs. He probably thought I was a hotel concierge or a bellhop captain, but instead of becoming offended and lashing out, I took it. Because he was an important man and I knew President Salinas wanted to meet him.

In fact, I was due to bring him to meet the president at 5:00 p.m., but I was so busy with all the other arrivals that I forgot. At 6:00 p.m., after I returned to my hotel room, it dawned on me how badly I'd screwed up. It was the scariest moment of my political life so far, and I was sure I would be fired. I had that feeling that you get in your stomach, when you know you failed spectacularly and there's nothing you can do but await the pain. With my guts churning, I changed clothes, and went downstairs to accept my fate. I expected to be met by the president's furious chief of staff, and I was, but he wasn't angry with me.

"Can you believe that *pinche* asshole," he said, referencing the minister from Japan, "He canceled the meeting with the President!"

I couldn't help but smile inside. That rude bastard saved my ass.

The economic summit only whet Salinas' and Serra's appetite for firm international trade agreements, and the first one that became real was NAFTA. After Bush lost the White House to Clinton in 1992, there was some concern that the NAFTA agreement that Serra had been negotiating for nearly three years would be abandoned. As a Democrat, Clinton was supported by labor unions who were opposed to the agreement on the assumption that manufacturing jobs would be lost to Mexico (they eventually would be). But in early 1993, Clinton re-engaged our administration in NAFTA talks.

On the day it was up to Congress to pass or reject a bill giving President Clinton and his administration the right to finalize negotiations with our team on the finer points of the deal, Mexico City streets were quiet. Everyone was glued to the television, awaiting an outcome which would have a profound effect on our markets. Not everyone in Mexico was in favor of NAFTA. The Mexican left worried about the way our energy, oil, food systems, and the environment would be compromised as a result of the agreement, but when the bill passed on Capitol Hill, one thing was certain: Mexico's economy would change forever.

Salinas hosted a celebratory dinner, and Serra was the guest of honor, but I wasn't invited, which was fine with me. I had to be up at 4:00 a.m. the next morning. I had an Ironman triathlon on my race calendar, and I wasn't going to miss a day of training.

On my ride through Mexico City that morning, I saw the future. Competition and investment would redraw the Mexican map and rearrange the face of our great city. Within months, American, European, and Japanese cars would pour across the border, along with personal computers, stereo systems, and other electronics, and that was just the beginning.

It was time to shake off the last vestiges of the closed economy that had dominated Mexico for generations. We were due for a software update. We were becoming a young, urban, creative and vibrant country, but we weren't yet global. Fortunately, a technocratic future was coming, and I was ready to be a part of it.

Every marathon

swim has at least

one crisis point,

some crucible the

swimmer must

navigate, a test

they must pass.

7

The Catalina Channel

Catalina Island, a rock floating in the Pacific Ocean, rests 32.3 kilometers off the coast of Southern California, and it has lived several lives. It was once a seasonal fishing camp for Native Californians until, like most of California's Channel Islands, it became the domain of Russian fur traders who battered fur seals to near extinction for profit. Then in the early 20th century, a self-made chewing gum magnate bought most of it and turned one half into a casino resort, and the other into a sheep and cattle ranch. On clear days in Los Angeles, you can see Catalina from just about any beach, which means that you can also see the Catalina Channel, the only channel in all of North America among the Oceans Seven.

I know Catalina well. It was the site of my biggest open water swimming failure, and it's where I've sought redemption ever since. Whenever I think of my most challenging endurance events in my entire career, my mind travels back in time and space to its cold, swirling, sharky waters.

Before the 1920's, nobody outside of southern California knew much about Catalina. But in 1919, William Wrigley Jr., a working-class kid turned chewing gum millionaire and owner of the Chicago Cubs, was looking for a place to escape the harsh winters of the Windy City and someone showed him pictures of Catalina Island and its 197 square kilometers of rugged, undeveloped paradise. That same day he bought most of the island for around $3 million.

Wrigley built an estate above the harbor for he and his wife, as well as a casino and a luxury hotel to lure weekenders. He created a ferry service to serve his tourism business and build real estate demand for residential plots he was selling to fellow snowbirds. In subsequent years, he added an exotic bird park and built a golf course. He even had his Cubs work out in Catalina during Major League Baseball spring training and built an exact replica of Chicago's Wrigley Field to serve as their home away from home.

But tourism continued to languish outside peak tourist season, and Wrigley was eager to build interest in his beloved island, so in 1926 he stared at the open ocean spread before him and hatched a plan. Like millions of others, Wrigley had been captivated by Gertrude Ederle's attempt to become the first woman to swim across the English Channel earlier that year. Although this was still a world without the X Games, and certainly without snowboarding, skateboarding or motocross,

Americans were already very much captivated by extreme behavior and adventure sports.

Marathon dances were trendy, so was plunging over Niagara Falls in a barrel, and when Ederle was successful in the English Channel, she became a big celebrity in the United States. For months, the media tracked her whereabouts. She gave President Coolidge swimming lessons and was given her own ticker tape parade in her native New York City.

Inspired by Ederle's feat and the attention she generated, Wrigley decided to hold an open water swim to show off Catalina. Except this wouldn't be a solo marathon swim. The Wrigley Ocean Marathon would be a proper race from Catalina Island to Point Vicente in San Pedro, California with dozens of athletes crossing the channel all at once.

Or so he hoped.

He offered Ederle $25,000 to participate and another $25,000 if she won. She eventually declined, but several other prominent swimmers, including Olympic medalists, did sign on. Each time another joined the field, the press ate it up, never failing to write about the beauty of Catalina whenever they filed their stories.

It was a cruel joke to stage the race in the middle of winter, when ocean temperatures can plummet to 12-15°C, but that's what Wrigley did because it was the downtime in his tourism calendar, and winter in Catalina is exactly what he hoped to promote. And it worked. Just by staging the race, Wrigley managed to embed Catalina into the mainstream American mind.

In the weeks leading up to the event, the American national press reported on the athletes. Their training was tracked, their backstories told. Few if any reporters, however, focused on 17-year-old George Young, a poor kid from Toronto who gave up his amateur status and a possible future Olympic berth to have a chance at winning $25,000 to care for his ailing mother.

On January 15th, 1927, 102 swimmers gathered on the shore where they were smeared with grease to protect them from the cold. Or so they thought. All the participants were assigned a boat of their own, where their coach could watch them and pass along food and drink, without touching their swimmer. Those same rules apply today. There were also Coast Guard boats with medical teams ready to respond to emergency and Wrigley chartered passenger boats to act as floating grandstands so spectators could follow the race from shore to shore. The biggest fear Wrigley and his staff had was that one of the athletes might drown, but there were so many boats in the water that day it would have been impossible for anyone to drown without someone noticing.

The gun went off at 11:24 a.m., and Young led from the start. He grew up swimming in the icy, freshwater lakes of Ontario, Canada, and was conditioned for the cold. Everyone else? Not so much. By sunset, he was 1.5 kilometers ahead of his closest competition. By 9:00 p.m. there were just twelve people left in the entire field.

When he was only a few kilometers from the mainland shore, he encountered a wall of current that held him in place. He swam with everything he had and still didn't move. It's a feeling I know well and have experienced dozens of times. When he did start moving ever so slowly forward, his swim trunks got caught in a patch of kelp. Once again, he was powerless to move, so he simply tore his trunks off and let them float away. At 3:08 a.m., he staggered ashore, naked, the first to swim across the Catalina Channel. When they heard he'd made it, and captured the prize, everyone else in the field dropped out. Young was the only person to finish that day.

Wrigley continued to hold the race for a few more years before abandoning it, but the channel remains etched into the collective consciousness of swimmers all over the world who pass along word of George Young and the harsh waters of the Catalina Channel from generation to generation. In the late 1990s, those stories found me. As of July 12th, 1999, ninety men and women had made a successful crossing, and I hoped to become number ninety-one.

This wasn't exactly my first rodeo. As I mentioned, I attempted the Catalina Channel for the first time in 1998, as part of my preparation for the English Channel, and that swim was an utter disaster. We shoved off from Long Beach harbor after dark and the swell was so choppy that when I went below deck for my required briefing, I wound up getting severe seasickness. Jumping into the water after midnight didn't help matters. Swimming in the chop only made things worse. I vomited constantly, became severely dehydrated and borderline hypothermic, and after four hours I gave into the conditions and gave up my quest. I was an utter failure, and when we arrived back on land part of me wondered if I had what it took to become a great open water swimmer.

In July 1999, those same questions lingered and in August I was due to swim the English Channel for the first time, which is why I returned to Catalina the month before. Nora thought it was a mistake. In her mind, if I failed again, the English Channel would be even more difficult for me mentally. Plus, by mid-July, I should have been tapering, not taking on a challenge as monumental as Catalina. Even if I were successful, such a demanding swim was sure to take a lot out of me and it was anybody's guess if I'd recover in time to deliver another all-out effort off the coast of Dover.

Those weren't the only stakes. Remember, before the Oceans Seven, the pinnacle of our sport was the Triple Crown of Open Water Swimming, which consists of the English Channel, a complete circumnavigation of Manhattan Island in New York, and the Catalina Channel. Much like the Oceans Seven, the Triple Crown was conceived as a way to build visibility for the sport of open water swimming, and the first to complete it was Alison Streeter. I'd already managed Manhattan, and if I could complete Catalina and follow it up with a successful English Channel swim, I would become just the eighth to ever do it.

This time there would be no rough water night cruise. I took the ferry to Catalina the day before and spent the night on the island. Or part of the night, anyway. I woke up at 3:00 a.m., with six hours of rest under my belt, to stretch and get ready for a 4:00 a.m. start.

The wind was mild when I boarded my support boat in Avalon harbor and we shoved off. Nora rubbed zinc on my body to protect me from the sun, and we were going over my feeding plan one last time when we passed a sailboat anchored in the bay, with a half dozen people partying deep into the night. Here I was going out for a 12-hour swim, and they were drinking and dancing. As we motored by them on our way to the starting point, three of the women took off their tops and flashed us. We laughed and waved, then turned north. A few minutes later we were idling off Long Point, the closest point to the Southern California coast. I slipped into the water just after 4:00 a.m.

The early hours were relatively easy, and even after dawn spread over the distant Southern California coastline, the current felt neutral and the wind light. It wasn't exactly warm water, but the temperature was roughly 17°C, which was warm enough for me. Things changed that afternoon. The wind kicked up the swell, and instead of carving dimpled glass, I flailed on an ocean teeter totter that kept pushing me north of Port Vicente. This wasn't a problem in terms of the swim being certified as a true crossing, but it meant that I would have to swim a lot further than 32.3 kilometers.

It was all very disorienting and dizzying. I worried about sea sickness and was concerned for my progress and my ability to endure the extra mile or two it would take. Meanwhile, my tongue was swollen with saltwater and I still had 16 kilometers to swim, at least.

I kept fighting, was soon enveloped by a favorable current, and within a few hours, I could see the shore loom closer and closer. Which was around the same time Nora spotted a shark about 25 meters in front of me. She didn't alert me because I was making great progress and she wanted my mind focused on the task at hand, but she and the rest of my team kept a close eye on that shark and discussed pulling me from the ocean. When the shark disappeared, they nervously watched the surface, pondering where or how it might reappear. It never did.

Through it all, I remained oblivious as I hammered toward the rolling waves crashing on a beach in the distance. At around 4:30 p.m., I felt my fingers graze the sandy bottom and staggered to my feet, in knee high tides. Usually when you swim in from Catalina, you land on a cobblestone beach on the Palos Verdes Peninsula, but the current had shoved us north to the crescent of wide, soft, golden sand that forms the southern end of Redondo Beach. I'd been swimming for 12 hours and 25 minutes when I walked slowly toward the tide line, and with my toes dry, waved toward my support boat. Its horn blared in triumph.

Before I had a chance to swim back to my team, a surfer called out. He and three of his buddies had watched me finish as they waxed their boards preparing for a surf session.

"Where did you come in from?" He asked.

"Catalina," I answered with a smile.

"Bullshit!" They responded in unison. I shrugged and laughed.

"Look at the boat." I pointed toward my team who were lined up along the railing and cheering for me. As soon as they saw them, those surfers started clapping too. They dropped their boards and took turns shaking my hand and patting me on the back.

A little more than a month later, I crossed the English Channel. At the time, I thought I was done with open water swimming. I was 40 years old and I'd completed the Triple Crown. There was no Oceans Seven yet. There was nothing more to chase in the open water, so I turned my focus back to triathlons.

Until I turned 50 years old.

By the summer of 2008, I was already a five-time Ironman. Ironman triathlons are full-day races that begin with a 3.86-kilometer swim, followed by a 180-kilometer bike ride and a 42.2-kilometer run. Any single stage of a race like that would exhaust most weekend warriors. Doing them non-stop one after another is the domain of only the most serious endurance athletes. Not that I was competitive for titles or age group medals. I was in it for the fun and the challenge alone. In fact, because I was still one of the better swimmers in the entire field, my Ironman triathlons shared the same ridiculous rhythm.

I always finished the swim with the pros, the real athletes, but as I transitioned to the bike it didn't take long for the professional men to pass me. Within a few kilometers, the pro women would pass me. Then all the younger amateur men, followed by the young women. Then men from my own age group passed me and several women, of course. All of them looked super fit, as if training for triathlons was their full-time job. On the run, there were always a few men, and at least one woman, who seemed to have even more body fat than I did that would pass me. The only thing that could heal that pain was passing one person. Just one, please God, just one!

The point is, in my body, mind, heart, and soul, I've always been a swimmer, and the stats tend to back that up. In 2008, I saw a challenge that nobody had ever thought to accomplish. I wanted to become the first person to complete the Triple Crown of Open Water Swimming twice. This time, I would do all three swims within a calendar year: the year I turned 50 years old.

The easiest of those three swims is invariably the Manhattan Island circumnavigation, but even though I'd done Manhattan twice before, I was still asked to apply to the Manhattan Swim Association to prove that I was capable. That meant I needed to have a swim of six hours or longer on my application within the past calendar year. I didn't have that and Catalina didn't have that requirement, so I opted to swim Catalina first and use that as my qualification swim for Manhattan.

When I slipped into the water at midnight on October 13th, 2008, my attempt to swim the Catalina Channel for just the 197th time in its history began. Conditions were bad from the outset. The water hovered around 15.5°C, which was unseasonably cold, and the coldest water I'd ever experienced. The wind was cold too, and the chop was horrible. I'd taken Bonine Non-Drowsiness on the boat ride out to stave off seasickness and I had a glow stick clipped to my Speedo. This was vital because the swell rose as high as two meters, which meant I was riding a bucking bronco up and down, yo-yoing four meters between peak and trough, all night long.

Along to support my swim was Nora, as usual, as well as Ricardo González (now one of the coaches for Mexico's national triathlon team), and my cardiologist Hermes Ilarraza. He was a new addition and I invited him along because during a recent check up, I'd been diagnosed with high blood pressure, which put me at a higher risk for a heart attack or stroke. We got it under control with medication, but the diagnosis hit Nora hard. She already had one death on her hands—Fausta's—and more recently had a second scary moment when one of her swimmers passed out after a long swim, though she was revived. To convince her to coach me in 2008, I had to bring my cardiologist along, and rent a defibrillator he could use to revive me if the worst happened.

For the first few hours, I swam between Ricardo, who was my kayaker, and my support boat, which was typical protocol in the Catalina Channel. Ricardo had all my water bottles and Accel energy gels. He was in charge of my feedings, but in the bracing wind and cold water I couldn't warm up no matter how hard I swam, and then in the third hour, Ricardo was broadsided by a swell and capsized.

Channel swimming rules dictated that I couldn't help him mount his kayak. If I touched him or his kayak, my swim would be disqualified. Meanwhile, all of my water bottles and gels were spilled all around us and drifting away. At least he was in a wetsuit. I was freezing in my Speedo, yet had to tread water in place until he could get sorted out. All of it took way too long, and I could feel the cold begin to take root in my body and mind.

Part of the reason the cold was getting to me on that swim was because I was very thin. I still had the body of an Ironman. I hadn't packed on my marine mammal layers of fat, which I lovingly call my bioprene. Plus, I hadn't prepared for the cold in any way, and my penalty was the worst six hours of my swimming life. My head pounded, my hands and feet ached. I was utterly exhausted.

My suffering peaked at 4:30 a.m. The sky was still black and the water dark and freezing. My hands felt frozen in place. I could barely bend them, and they hurt like fucking hell. I swam over to my support boat. Nora leaned toward me. I didn't like confessing pain to her or anyone else but given all the grief she gave me after my blood pressure diagnosis, I figured she wanted me to err on the side of caution. Plus, I didn't want to keep my true feelings from my coach.

"I feel very bad," I said, through trembling blue lips. "It's the worst I've ever felt in the water."

"Oh, I'm sorry," Nora said, in an annoyed voice. We locked eyes and I could feel her stare through me as she raised her voice. "Did you think this was going to be easy?!"

Hypothermia continued to nip at me from behind, nibbling away at my body and mind, but it couldn't stop me.

I was looking for empathy and instead got tough love from the same woman who required me to bring a cardiologist along to guarantee her participation. I'd expected her to coddle me. Instead, she called me out, and pissed me off, but something funny happened. My anger warmed me up and gave me a jolt of power. Six hours is all I needed to qualify for Manhattan, and in her mind I still had 90 more minutes to swim before she would allow me to give in and quit. Oh yes, Nora knew what she was doing.

I remember getting to hour six. It was just after 6:00 a.m., and the sky was brightening, but I was still so cold that I was beginning to cramp up, which is always a danger sign. David Clark, the president of the Catalina Channel Swimming Association, had taken over as my kayaker due to the difficult conditions, and he was a great paddler, very easy to follow, but he also kept a close watch on me. When I swam over to get a drink at the bottom of the hour, he looked into my eyes to gauge if I had begun to succumb to hypothermia, which, as we know, can be deadly.

"What day is it?" He asked. I sipped my water, swallowed and paused. "What day did you start swimming?"

I knew this was a test, and that if I didn't have the answers he might pull me, but I was so cold and tired I was having trouble remembering exactly what day it was. Part of me wanted to continue to swim and pretend I hadn't heard him. Instead, I took a guess.

"It's Tuesday, and I started at midnight on Tuesday." I didn't know if I was right or not, but I knew for sure that my voice sounded shredded with uncontrollable shivers. He didn't say anything at first. He continued to evaluate me. Finally, he nodded, and I took off swimming.

Within minutes the sun rose, spreading its warmth across the surface of the sea. The sun brings energy and hope to an open water swimmer who has been pushing all night long, and with the light, I could see the coastline moving closer and closer. There was a wildfire in the hills around Los Angeles that year. We could see the flames, and the smoke rising like a mushroom cloud over the city. The water itself was still cold, and I had much work left to do, but the waves relented enough that I was able to make solid progress and as I found my rhythm, I was overtaken by a stampeding pod of common dolphins. They surrounded me and swam along with me for at least a half hour, and for the first time since we launched, I felt good about my chances.

Every marathon swim has at least one crisis point, some crucible the swimmer must navigate, a test they must pass. That night—that cold—was mine in 2008, and yet I made it through to the other side. Hypothermia continued to nip at me from behind, nibbling away at my body and mind, but it couldn't stop me.

Thirteen hours and ten minutes after launching from Catalina's Long Point, I swam toward the rocky shore on the Palos Verdes Peninsula. The waves were heavy that morning, especially for an exhausted swimmer with jelly legs, but I managed to crawl out off the water and onto the cobbles until my toes were dry. When the horn sounded, I slipped back into the water and swam to my support boat, which idled about 100 meters off shore. It was the most pleasant 100 meters of the entire day.

My team helped me out of the water and huddled around me. My body was chafed, and my bones rattled as I struggled to warm up. I was wrapped in warm towels then my robe, and handed a steaming cup of hot chocolate as we started toward Long Beach Harbor, just 15 minutes away. That's when David Clark, a Catalina Channel legend with decades of experience as a swimmer, paddler and observer on scores of solo and relay attempts, approached me with a knowing smile.

"You had the most difficult day in the entire season," Clark said, "and one of the worst I've ever seen." He held his hand out and I took it. "Congratulations."

That swim qualified me for Manhattan and the English Channel, both of which I knocked off the following summer to become the first to complete the Triple Crown twice. At the time, I considered my Triple Crown year to be the pinnacle of my swimming achievements. I'd accomplished a world's first and figured I was done with open water swimming and triathlons too. I got into mountaineering, learned how to be a technical climber, and dreamed of Everest. But for soul swimmers—the mad ones that need it even more than they want it consciously—the pull of the ocean can be strong, much stronger than any current or riptide.

The only way to

demonstrate I had

that faith was to

step into the waters

of uncertainty and

embrace risk one

more time.

8

Adrift

People who were there said the gun appeared out of nowhere.

It was March 23rd, 1994 when presidential candidate Luis Donaldo Colosio arrived in the Lomas Taurinas neighborhood of Tijuana, a steep, eroding canyon studded with plywood shacks and cheap cinderblock *casitas*. The streets were only half-paved, the fencing cobbled from spent bedsprings. Flanked by bodyguards, he climbed onto the bed of a pick-up truck, his stump in this place of need, to provide hope and make a case for both the status quo and something entirely new. Talk about a difficult needle to thread.

Colosio was a PRI man, one of the most powerful members of Mexico's ruling party that had run the country for 65 years, yet in a famous speech he had given a few weeks before his visit to Tijuana, he spoke of tearing away at the roots of authoritarianism. It was terrain he'd been trending toward once he began to figure out how drastically and swiftly Mexico's political currents had shifted since his official nomination to the presidency the previous December.

Colosio had been instrumental to the success of President Salinas, who helped rebuild the economy from the rubble of devaluation and made NAFTA real. On the night of Colosio's nomination, the country was politically and economically stable, and his victory seemed assured.

Then the peasant uprising in Chiapas happened. The Zapatistas, rural rebels who thought themselves the second coming of Mexico's original revolutionaries, seized control of the streets in San Cristóbal de las Casas and other municipalities in Chiapas on January 1st. Not long after there were a series of bombings in Mexico City, and it seemed to the average Mexican that our stability had eroded overnight. Colosio's campaign, which kicked off on January 10th, was largely overshadowed and ignored.

Stories were printed in papers across the country questioning whether he would even make it to the election. He didn't read them because he was too busy trying to figure out what to do. He knew that to gain visibility and eventually win he would have to talk about changing the system, which meant he had to forge an ideological split from his mentor, President Salinas.

In his famous, controversial, and popular March 6th speech, he seized on themes first raised by the Zapatistas themselves. He spoke of indigenous rights, governmental abuse, and an increasingly democratized Mexico. With that speech, he unofficially cut ties with Salinas and found an effective message, which he brought with him to Tijuana. Confident and energized by surging poll numbers, he didn't travel in a large entourage or with a massive security footprint. He loved people and thrived on the populist energy surging around him. As part of his campaign management team—I was in charge of finances—I saw it a few times. Although, to be fair, I was not with him on March 23rd. I wasn't there to see him gather the crowd into the palm of his hand, stir them up, then wade into them with genuine affection.

After he was done speaking, he hopped down from the bed of the pick up and pressed toward all the arms reaching out while a Banda tune blared. It was one of those electric political moments. His smile beamed, his supporters called his name, and nobody saw the assassin extend his arm over the shoulder of a Colosio bodyguard as the candidate passed by. Even on the footage it's impossible to tell where the pistol came from or who's holding it, as the muzzle moves forward, hovering just above Colosio's ear, before the violent flash.

The candidate slumped onto the half-paved street, bleeding from the head. The crowd scattered as his bodyguards rushed him to his Suburban, which sped toward the nearest hospital. Not that it did any good. At 6:55 p.m. on March 23rd, Luis Donaldo Colosio was pronounced dead. The would-be president of Mexico had been assassinated.

Minutes after the shooting, while I was sitting in my office with some colleagues on the Colosio campaign, my video phone rang. I'd bought it so I could see Ximena's face whenever she called, and only she and one or two others had that number. If it rang, I knew it was either my daughter or it was an emergency. One of the few who had access to that phone was Juan Carlos Téllez, a member of my staff who had been on site with Colosio in Tijuana.

"They just shot Colosio," he said. The statement sounded so ridiculous I laughed out loud. I figured he was using my emergency number as a practical joke. In those pre-social media days, news didn't travel in real time. Video evidence wasn't broadcast by onlookers live and direct. In the 1990's, during any breaking news situation, it still took at least some time to sort out what happened, when and where.

"Don't give me that shit, Juan Carlos," I said, "If you want to stay in Tijuana, just say so."

"No, Antonio," he replied in a grave tone. "They just shot Colosio."

I buzzed Ernesto Zedillo immediately. Zedillo was Colosio's campaign manager, and my boss. He'd heard the news too, and like me, assumed it had to be a joke.

"I don't think it's a joke, Ernesto," I said. He sighed deeply. "Come up to my office," he said.

I sprinted up three flights of stairs to the 12th floor, but by the time I arrived in his office, breathless, Zedillo was on his mammoth cellphone speaking to another of Colosio's campaign staff who had called in from Tijuana. That's when the red phone on his desk, a hotline with direct access to only the president of Mexico, began ringing off the hook.

If Colosio was a bigger-than-life political star, and he was, Ernesto Zedillo was his opposite number. He was just as committed to growing Mexico into a modern political and economic force, but his style was more conservative, perhaps a little stiff, and far less showy. What made him a tremendous campaign manager was his work ethic. Nobody would ever outwork Ernesto Zedillo, and his discipline would soon reshape his future in ways even he couldn't imagine while staring that red phone down.

He caught my eye and gestured for me to answer. During my five years working under Serra at the Ministry of Trade, I'd spoken to President Salinas many times, but he never sounded anything like this. His voice shook with distress. At first, I had trouble understanding him, but then the truth started to sink in. I nodded, and Zedillo took the phone from my hand as I sunk into the nearest chair. Our would-be president was dead, and the election was in just ten weeks.

An arrest was made that day. Mario Aburto Martínez, the gunman, would be convicted and sentenced to over 40 years in prison. He claimed he acted alone, but few in Mexico were satisfied with the police findings or his conviction. In fact, the Colosio assassination became Mexico's version of the JFK murder. Like the Zapruder film, footage from Tijuana was played repeatedly on a loop. In some circles, it still is.

Theories were hatched, would-be guilty parties named on white boards in news rooms and the bulletin boards of conspiracy theorists from Chiapas to Juarez. Not even Salinas was spared from suspicion. Colosio's March 6th speech was an indictment of Salinas, conspiracy advocates like to say, as well as a proclamation against drug cartels that were starting to inflict major damage in Mexico.

Was any of that true? I've always been clueless and perhaps a little naive when it comes to Mexico's cartel problem, but it's quite a stretch to believe that one speech is motive enough for the president to conspire in an assassination of the candidate he had handpicked to be his successor. Plus, I know how Salinas sounded that night. He was shocked to his core and overcome with grief. To this day, even with the material murderer imprisoned and thoroughly investigated, there are those who insist that the assassination was not an act of one man alone.

All of Mexico mourned that night, but those of us in the campaign war room were well aware that our grief was only part of our burden. We also needed to find a new candidate as soon as possible. Into that vacuum stepped Ernesto Zedillo, Colosio's best friend, campaign manager, and speechwriter.

Zedillo was born in Mexico City in 1951. His father was an electrician and his mother a tireless woman who worked to support her family from age 14 until she died at 38. Among other jobs, she was a nurse—she went to medical school for three years—and a secretary. When Ernesto was three years old, the family moved to the border town of Mexicali. Later, the young Zedillo returned to the capital to continue his education at the National Polytechnic Institute. In the meantime, he worked first at Banjército, the bank of the army, and later at the Ministry of the Presidency. His boss, prominent economist Leopoldo Solís, encouraged him to do a PhD at Yale University. After graduation, he was recruited by the Bank of Mexico, where he remained for a decade, until then President Miguel de la Madrid appointed him as

Undersecretary at the Ministry of Programming and Budget. At the beginning of the Salinas administration in 1988, when he was just 36 years old, he was chosen to lead that agency. Then, in 1992, Salinas appointed him Minister of Education, but he resigned nearly two years later to run Colosio's campaign.

Zedillo's resignation worked in his favor because according to our constitution, only those who have not served in high public office in the six months prior to the election are eligible to run. That put him on a short list of candidates to succeed Colosio. The PRI's Political Committee approved him as our candidate the very next week.

As a campaign, we had a ton of ground to cover across Mexico to introduce our new candidate to a country that had scarcely heard of him, so that's exactly what we did. As a former Undersecretary at the Trade Ministry, I had a network of business contacts (in both small and large companies) across the republic and our strategy was to get local businessmen to spread the Zedillo, technocratic gospel. I was still Campaign Controller. Just like during the Colosio campaign, I was responsible for any and all campaign expenditures, but I was also responsible for voting districts in ten states throughout Mexico. I traveled, networked, and campaigned for Zedillo seven days a week.

Of course, it was Ernesto Zedillo himself who captured the country's imagination. He'd always been a great policy man and a terrific speechwriter, but he had never shown much interest or aptitude for the microphone prior to his candidacy, and his initial speeches weren't met with much enthusiasm. They sounded like university lectures rather than stirring political rally cries, but with practice, he found his form and began dazzling crowds. Soon enough his poll numbers began to rise.

The menace of Colosio's assassination, however, did not fade. While on the campaign trail, I got a call from our headquarters and was ordered back to Mexico City. I was met by two armed bodyguards at the gate. They escorted me from the airport to the campaign offices where Esteban Moctezuma, Zedillo's campaign manager, and General Roberto Miranda, Zedillo's chief of security, were waiting for me.

"A series of raids were conducted this week, Antonio," Miranda said, "and our agents found a list of PRI officials who we suspect have been targeted for kidnapping. You're one of them."

I stared at them in disbelief. I was a behind-the-scenes guy I made connections, helped get deals done, but I was a cog. I never operated the levers of the machine, and to my knowledge I had no real political enemies.

"No," I pushed back. "Nobody even knows who I am."

"You're handling the money. They know that. So, we have to protect you. We can't lose anybody else."

From then on, I couldn't drive myself anywhere. No matter where I was or what I wanted to do, I now required two bodyguards and a bulletproof car. It was terrifying.

By then, I was divorced. Mónica and I split up two years after Ximena was born, in 1991. The fact that Ximena lived with her mother during the week helped me relax because I knew she was safe, but it was still nerve-racking being surrounded by armed bodyguards day and night, especially with my lifestyle.

180

I'd gotten used to early mornings and late nights. I woke up before sunrise each morning to ride or run, and then worked all day before spending late nights in bars and clubs. I was cutting loose, developing a lifelong friendship with Herradura Blanco and becoming close with the maître d's at all the best restaurants in Mexico City. Now, wherever I went, I was shadowed by armed men and a reminder that my life was in perpetual danger, which was usually enough to send me home early.

Mexico's 1994 presidential election was held on August 21st, and by then we knew Zedillo was a lock to win. But when you work in the apparatus of politics, once victory in a given election is secured, the stress doesn't fade. If anything, it magnifies because working on a victorious campaign doesn't guarantee anybody except the candidate a job in the new administration.

At the victory party there were hugs and kisses everywhere, and Zedillo delivered a stirring speech. "There are no losers," he said, "All of us, in the future, have a task and a responsibility to fulfill." As for where my responsibility would lie, however, I left the celebration uncertain.

When I jumped to the Colosio campaign from the Salinas administration, I took a big risk. I'd given up my job under Jaime Serra at the Trade Ministry, in part to escape his long shadow and to prove myself. Had we lost, that stench of defeat would have stuck to me like bad fish. I knew that going in, but by then, I was comfortable with risk.

"Don't fear failure, Toño, fear mediocrity."

That is what my father told me when I was just seven years old. Though he'd become a shell of the man I'd once idolized, his words were with me when I made the leap. It was comfortable in Serra's shadow. It would have been easy to stay there, but I was looking for more. Just as I had been during high school when I was still dazzled by my Olympic dreams. I followed that dream and I failed, but that didn't make me a failure. The moves I made to leave the comfort of my life in Mexico and challenge myself to grow was the main reason I was working under Serra in the first place, and I knew that same cosmic domino effect could work in my favor again.

Settling into a position on the campaign was like the beginning of a marathon swim. Success was not a guarantee, but I had to trust in myself that I had the strength to endure no matter the conditions. The only way to demonstrate that faith was to step into the waters of uncertainty and embrace risk one more time.

On election night, it seemed my risk had paid off. It certainly should have. We were victorious and I had been one of the campaign's most valuable contributors. In my mind, that warranted consideration for a top post in the administration, yet for months I watched Zedillo summon my colleagues, people who weren't even a part of his campaign, for private interviews.

Jaime Serra was appointed to become Finance Minister, and several others I knew were anointed with top jobs in the incoming Zedillo administration, while I remained on the fringes waiting for the phone to ring. Sure, I still had a secretary and an office, but we had almost nothing to do other than listen to the rumor mill.

It's an interesting thing to go from the fulcrum of a campaign, when everyone needed me and wanted to get in touch with me—because I had the keys to the safe—to living a life in near anonymity. The silence was as deafening as it was concerning. I would joke with my brothers—they were the only people I could discuss this with—that I was so irrelevant nobody would ever even think to kidnap me anymore. And sure enough, my bulletproof car was repossessed, my bodyguards reassigned.

Finally, four months after Zedillo's victory, the lease on our campaign offices ran out. Everyone but me had already cleared their desks and moved on, so it was up to me to lock up and turn in the keys without any idea what I might do next. I was a divorcee with a two-year-old daughter to help raise and pay for, and I had no job. In fact, I was forced to sell some of my assets to get liquidity.

The frustrating weeks turned to anxious months and I took out my angst in the pool. Swimming helped channel my energies in a productive way. Running and cycling helped too. In the absence of a role to play in government, I dedicated myself to training for my first Ironman, but even that wasn't enough for me. I was used to living a full life, packed with both sports and politics. Now, I just felt empty.

The week before Zedillo's inauguration, I went to see Jaime Serra. I'd emerged from his shadow for less than a year only to seek his shelter once more. His office in San Ángel, the seat of financial power for all of Mexico, buzzed with life. Phones rang in a call and response symphony floating

183

over the percussion of keyboards and coffee cups. Wood heels and hard leather soles clicked and clacked on polished wood floors, and here I was entering the scene from pure oblivion.

I followed a secretary in a fitted business suit toward the corner office, where I found Jaime Serra standing at his desk. He waved me to a leather arm chair to wait while he finished up a phone call. After he hung up, he sat at his desk and looked me up and down.

"You look fit, Antonio. Very fit," he said.

I opted not to tell him about the Ironman. I hated having to call for this meeting in the first place and hoped to share as little as possible. I'd say enough to leave the room with a job and nothing more.

"I have a lot of time on my hands," I said. He nodded.

"I'm aware," he said.

"It's not fair," I said, then cringed inside. I sounded like a frustrated loser. He shrugged.

"I don't know what to tell you, Antonio. You left the Ministry."

"You gave me your blessing to go work on the campaign. I did it to help the party and to show you all the things I can do."

"I know what you can do. I've always known." He was obviously waiting for me to ask for help. It was time to bite the bullet.

"Okay then, I want to be the general director of Nacional Financiera." That was a top position in the Mexican financial sector. Serra shook his head.

"No, you cannot do that. The last guy left the bank with a $12 billion hole. Knowing you, you'll increase it because all your businessmen friends will come asking for loans."

"Then let me be your Undersecretary of Spending. I can distribute money to the federal and state governments. I know people in every state. That's an empty seat. Let me fill it for you." Serra shook his head again.

"No. You have too many friends who are governors. People will say you are playing favorites. It won't look good."

As we spoke, part of me was enraged at the lack of institutional memory, but I was also utterly deflated by the lack of support from one of my greatest friends and allies. Serra could see he knocked the wind out of my sails. He followed my eyes to the floor and played his hand.

"What I can offer you is the position of Undersecretary of Administration here at the Finance Ministry. I can use you here. Nobody runs an office like you." He was offering me the exact position I'd held before at the Ministry of Trade. It was a horizontal move, not a vertical leap. I raised my eyes toward his.

"Bathrooms," I said, remembering the first job he'd asked me to do. Make sure the bathrooms were clean. Tears of disappointment streamed down my cheeks.

"I'm afraid that's the best we can do."

I didn't accept his offer. At least not right away. I went home and considered how I could turn this mediocre turn of events into some sort of advantage. I knew that Serra's star was on the rise. He was being considered by higher-ups in the party as a future presidential candidate, and with no other offers, we both knew I had to accept. And I did, with one essential caveat: that the communications office, which handled public and media relations and communications with Congress, report to me, as well. He agreed, and the following

Monday I went to work, which gave me a front row seat to Mexico's worst financial crisis in a decade.

The Tequila Crisis hit Mexico hard just before Christmas in 1994, but the trouble began before Zedillo's inauguration on December 1st. Foreign investors had been getting squeamish about doing business in Mexico thanks, in part, to a *Wall Street Journal* article that questioned the country's ability to have enough cash on hand to pay its debts. Then, in mid-December, investors made their move.

The first big test of the Zedillo administration landed on Serra's desk, and in an effort to maintain stability in the Mexican stock market, he opted to devalue the peso against the dollar by 15%. That's not much, but it sent a terrible message and investors responded by selling off their pesos at a loss (which further devalued the currency) and pulling their money out of Mexican banks by the truck load.

Technically, I was in charge of all communication coming out of the Finance Ministry, but I found out by fax the next morning like everyone else on the sidelines of government. By the time I reached my office, the Mexican stock exchange was in free fall and the national bank faced certain default. In January, a nearly $50 billion bailout, administered by the IMF and organized by the Clinton administration, set us on a road toward stability, but that road was rough. Inflation rocked everyday people. Prices rose by one-third, thousands defaulted on their mortgages. Serra saw his error early and fell on the sword. He resigned in December 1994 and went back to Princeton to teach and lick his wounds. He would never work in the upper reaches of government again.

I managed to weather the crisis, in part because I wasn't involved with the response, but my days at the Finance Ministry were numbered. Zedillo would soon appoint Serra's replacement, who would hand pick his own undersecretaries.

I tried to get the president's attention to make my case to become second in command at the central export-import bank in Mexico. I needed a place to land and import-export had been my bread and butter since I was a kid. It seemed a natural fit, but Zedillo didn't have time to hear me out. He had a crisis on his hands, so I stayed on at the Finance Ministry, enduring the chaotic shit storm that was the Mexican economy, and hoped my next post would be revealed soon. In the meantime, I focused on the three things that brought me joy amidst the drama: my daughter, Ximena, my training, and my new girlfriend, Lucía.

We met prior to the presidential campaign, at a birthday party given by a friend in politics from Monterrey. It was held at a home in the Tlalpan neighborhood and called for 8 p.m. As usual, I was punctual. Everyone else was fashionably late. Even the host. When the host finally arrived home, he showed my lifelong friend Carlos López—who I'd known since my German School days—and me to a table in the center of the garden. We had a drink together, but as guests began to arrive, he left us to mingle.

This was an exclusive party, and as the space filled up with important people much higher up in government than I was, we were asked to move tables. The mucky-mucks kept rolling in and we were moved a second, then a third time. By the end of it, we were sitting on the edge of the party with views of a ramp that pedestrians walked up to reach the front door. At least that offered us a sneak peek of everyone who entered, from the waist down.

All the men wore suits and dress shoes, as if they just fled the office. Most women wore fashionable gowns and heels. I'd changed before leaving work and was wearing a turtleneck and a leather jacket. The point is, I stuck out, and so did she. She was wearing a mini skirt, and all I could see were her long legs, the best I'd ever seen. I looked over at Carlos and sighed.

"I must meet the owner of those legs," I said. He nodded and laughed.

Lucía Rangel almost didn't make it to the party that night. She lived in Monterrey but happened to be in Mexico City for work when she was invited by the guest of honor, Agustín Basave. Lucía asked her friend, Ana Lupe, to tag along, but when they drove up there was no parking. They circled the block several times to no avail, and almost went home, but the fates intervened with the perfect parking space.

She and Ana found a table across the garden, in a far corner near the bar, but were surrounded by people they didn't know, and once again contemplated leaving. I had no idea about any of this, of course. All I knew was that the more I watched her, the more I had to meet her, and when she left the table for the bathroom, I waded through the crowd to join the queue behind her.

"Do you belong to PRI?" I asked. She turned to me and laughed. All around glasses clinked, laughter and conversation merged into a toneless hum, as a storm of salsa music gathered overhead. It was all brass and hand drums. A singer lamented lost love.

"No way," she said.

"And why not?"

"I'm a psychoanalyst."

"What a coincidence! I'm also a therapist." She seemed skeptical, but I had a beard, was smoking a cigar, and looked the part. "Jungian," I said with a self-assured nod.

"I'm a Lacanian," she said. I touched her elbow, felt her warm skin for the first time, and with a gentle tug pulled her a half step closer. She looked down at my hand. I let go.

"You see that man there?" I pointed to a colleague from the Trade Ministry, Eloy Cantú, on his way to the bar. He was also from Monterrey, and I didn't realize that she knew him. "He's very famous."

"Him? Famous?"

"He has a very important job. The country would fall apart without him."

The bathroom door opened. It was her turn. She smiled, shook her head, and disappeared behind the door. When she returned from the bathroom I was chatting with Eloy, and she joined us. It turned out they grew up together. Eloy introduced me along with my job and title. He held the same position as I did, but in a different ministry, and she knew that.

"I knew you were in politics," she said with a smirk. "I suppose you are both famous."

"Very famous," I said. Eloy looked confused.

The three of us chatted casually for a few minutes. She was bubbly and friendly, and I was taken by her beauty and softness. Soon enough her friend joined us, along with the guest of honor, Agustín Basave. I could tell by the way he looked at her and spoke to her that Agustín was interested, but was the feeling between them mutual?

There was a lull in the conversation. Lucía and Ana shared a glance. "Shall we go?" Ana asked. Eloy, Agustín, and I begged them to stay. "Well, I have to go," Ana said, "but if one of you will drive her home..."

"I'll take you!" Like overeager puppies, Agustín and I both blurted it out at the same time. Ana and Eloy laughed. Lucía caught my eye and sighed as she turned to Agustín.

"Thank you very much," she said before turning back toward me once more. Our eyes met. "I accept, Antonio."

It wasn't until 4:00 a.m. when we finally slid into the back seat of Carlos' car. We were slightly drunk and leaned against one another, as he swerved through the streets of San Ángel toward Ana's house. I prayed for sharp, wrong turns. I didn't want the car ride to end.

When we arrived a few minutes later, I walked her to the door. We lingered on the steps and stared into one another's eyes. We were both divorced with children and lived busy lives in two different cities. We made no sense, I knew that. But I knew something else too. By the time she scribbled her phone number down, handed it to me, and closed the door behind her, I was already in love.

She flew home the next afternoon, and though I never asked her for her address, I did my homework, and by the time she arrived, there was a magnificent bouquet of fresh flowers waiting for her.

She was smart, kind and beautiful, and I saw her whenever I could during the campaign. I introduced her to Ximena, who was just three years old, and I met her 10-year-old son too. His name was David. We were still long distance during the first days of the Zedillo administration, and if anything made the wait for my new post bearable, it was Lucía.

I was rushing through the Mexico City airport late for my flight to see her one Friday night in February 1995, when my Nokia cell phone rang. I looked at the phone number and knew it was the president's chief of staff Liébano Sáenz. I dropped my bags and answered. It was the call I'd been waiting for ever since Serra resigned.

"Antonio, hold the line for President Zedillo."

I checked my watch. My plane was leaving in ten minutes and the phone reception was horrible, but the president was finally calling. One minute passed. Then two. The ground staff made the final boarding announcement and the president still hadn't picked up. I checked my phone. The line was still connected, then I heard static and the chief of staff picked up again.

"Apologies, Antonio, he has another call. Call us when you land in Monterrey."

I couldn't relax on the 80-minute flight. Every cell in my body brimmed with anticipation. When I landed, I caught a cab and as soon as Lucía opened the door to greet me, I told her I needed to use the phone. Once again, the president was unavailable. This time he was in a cabinet meeting.

"Don't worry, Antonio," Liébano told me, "Fausto Alzati, the Minister of Education will call you tonight with great news."

So that was it. I'd be working in education. I called around and learned that all the undersecretary positions at the Ministry of Education were already full. The only available job I could find was the ambassadorship to UNESCO in Paris.

Jacques Lacan, the famous French analyst, was Lucía's hero. To her, Paris is the center of the universe, and it's one of my favorite cities in the world. We spent the rest of the evening imagining our lives together in Paris. We saw ourselves walking through Montmartre in the rain, sipping wine and listening to jazz every evening, waking up to perfect croissant and coffee, and doing the hard work of visiting beautiful ruins—UNESCO heritage sites—all over the world. Dreaming that life together filled us both with romance and we fell into one another's arms and into bed. When we woke up bleary-eyed to the jarring cry of my cell phone, it all came crashing down.

"Antonio, I'd like to start by saying how excited I am to be working together. I know you are going to do a phenomenal job." It was Fausto Alzati. Lucía sat up in bed, listening in. We were giddy.

"Thank you, Fausto, I can't wait. I'd leave for Paris tomorrow if you want." There was an awkward pause on his end of the line.

"Paris? Who told you that you're going to Paris?" He asked, confused.

"Aren't I? The UNESCO post is unfilled so… I thought… I hoped…"

More silence.

"That's a meaningless post, Antonio. Anybody can do that. No, the president has appointed you to lead Conalep. He told me you are the only man for this job. We don't want you in Paris," he said. "We need you in Metepec."

Now it was my turn to go silent. Metepec was in the armpit of Central Mexico, two hours from my house, far from relevance in every direction. I'd never even heard of Conalep, had no idea what it stood for, and I'd spent my entire career in government. He could play up the urgency, appeal to my ego all he wanted, and he did continue delivering a sales pitch I was barely tuned into, but no matter what he said, I knew Metepec was in the boonies, and this Conalep sounded like career exile.

193

"Metepec." I cut him off. "You need me in… Metepec."

"*Sí, señor,*" he said. "*Por supuesto.*"

I thought I'd

seen and felt

almost everything

a body of water

can deliver, but

I'd never set foot

in Hawaii.

— Food break next to Dan Simonelli's kayak during my Catalina Channel swim —
PABLO ARGÜELLES CATTORI

— With Rafael Álvarez after the last training session before crossing the Catalina Channel —
MARÍA PAULA MARTÍNEZ JÁUREGUI LORDA

— *In the middle of the Strait of Gibraltar with Mariel Hawley, Nora Toledano, and Eduardo Rodríguez* —
PABLO ARGÜELLES CATTORI

— Enjoying Japanese hospitality and a tea ceremony after a training session in Tappi —
PABLO ARGÜELLES CATTORI

— *Meditating before my Tsugaru Strait crossing attempt* —
PABLO ARGÜELLES CATTORI

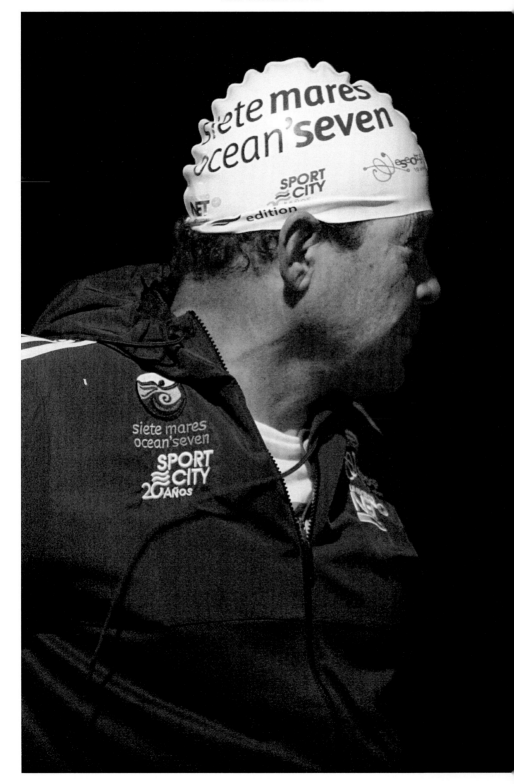

The moment Quinton Nelson informs me of the likelihood of going ahead with my North Channel crossing attempt —
PAULO NUNES DOS SANTOS

ith Lucía, looking at the **James and Frances Macfarlane,** *which would guide me during my North Channel crossing —*
PAULO NUNES DOS SANTOS

— Nora Toledano giving me instructions —
PABLO ARGÜELLES CATTORI

— Ariadna del Villar, Rafael Álvarez, and Nora Toledano —
PABLO ARGÜELLES CATTORI

— *The lighthouse near Portpatrick, Scotland* —

PABLO ARGÜELLES CATTORI

— *On the boat after my North Channel swim* —
PABLO ARGÜELLES CATTORI

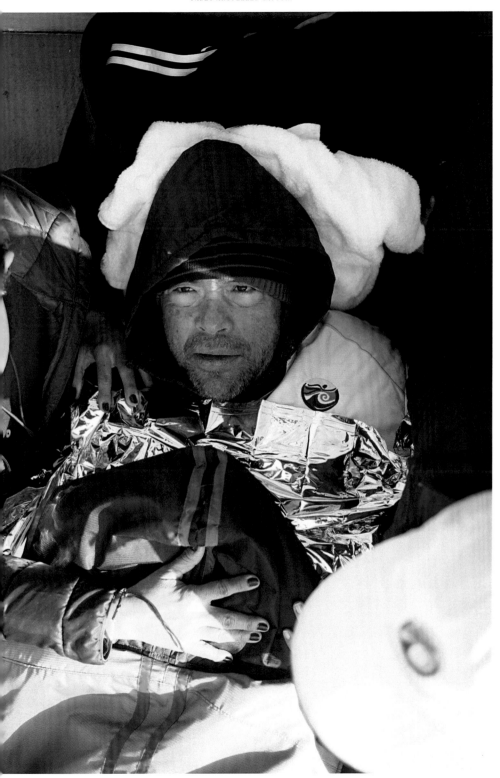

9

The Ka'iwi Channel

The echo of my Tsugaru triumph faded quickly. Two weeks after returning home, my left shoulder was still locked up. I couldn't so much as lift my left arm over my head, and in my condition there was absolutely no way I would be able to swim the Ka'iwi Channel, a turbulent 45-kilometer stretch of the Pacific Ocean connecting the Hawaiian Islands of Molokai and Oahu, in March 2016, as planned. I needed to find a solution, or my Oceans Seven dream was dead.

My Eureka moment struck during one of my rare strolls through Facebook, where I read of an Argentine trainer, an expert in range of motion, who had helped older swimmers overcome injury. The story was posted by Ricardo Durón, a trainer at Sport City, my gym in Coyoacán. I messaged him hoping to get in touch with the Argentine. Ricardo knew him well, and he gave me the contact, but he also mentioned that there was no reason for me to travel to Argentina when he could help me using those same techniques.

Like me, Ricardo had been an aspiring Olympic swimmer as a young man. His event was the 200m individual medley, and after competing at the college level in Mexico, when he was 23 years old he moved to San Luis Obispo, California, hoping stiffer competition and better coaching could enable him to make the 2000 Olympics in Sydney. Almost, but not quite. Just like me, he missed making the Mexican national team by one place.

He didn't give up. He kept competing, and soon became connected to Jack Roach, the coach for the Mexican national team, at a swim meet in Tijuana in 2001. Under Jack's tutelage, he switched to the breaststroke, and steadily improved his times, but at the 2004 Olympic trials, he again missed the cut by just one place. His double disappointment was one I could relate to more than most.

Eventually, he gravitated toward coaching and wound up at Sport City working with sponsored athletes of all kinds. On the side, he studied biomechanics, muscle alignment, resistance training and muscle activation techniques. Turns out there was nobody better in the world to restore my full range of motion and get me back in the water chasing the Oceans Seven.

Ricardo had developed a program using digital sensors that measure the force swimmers generate in the water, and on our first day working together, he put me through his paces. It didn't surprise either of us that after swimming just 300m, he could tell that almost all of my force was being generated by my right side. Most, if not all, swimmers have a strong side that they favor, but the more efficient their stroke, the more even their power from both sides, and the greater their speed. Because my left shoulder still ached terribly, I'd taken to favoring my right even more than usual, and the results had Ricardo shaking his head in disbelief.

"You must have an incredible will to succeed," he said while I toweled off.

"Why is that?" I asked.

"Because I can't believe you swam across the Tsugaru Strait with that stroke!" I started laughing because sometimes— most of the time—you just have to laugh at yourself to really enjoy any difficult process in life.

From then on, we did two to three Muscle Activation Techniques (MAT) sessions per week. It's a technique that falls somewhere between chiropractic treatment and massage in which Ricardo worked to reactivate muscles in my arms and back that were either underutilized or overworked. Then I'd get in the pool and he would give me guidance to refine my stroke, hoping to make me more efficient. He also brought in a terrific trainer, Rafael Álvarez, to improve my overall strength and conditioning.

To be perfectly candid, both Rafa and Ricardo were a bit shocked at my appearance when we first met. They'd heard about my athletic accomplishments, both recent and in the past, and they expected a specimen a bit more chiseled. When I told them about my dedicated workout regiment, starting at 4:30 a.m. six days a week, they were even more puzzled. Then I confessed my weakness for fine foods, Herradura Blanco, Napa Valley wines, Cuban cigars and single malt scotch, and they saw the light. They didn't like it, but I told them my

197

lifestyle would not change, and they would have to accept it. They shrugged, nodded, and urged me to drink more water. My muscles, fascia and joints would all work better if I was better hydrated, they said.

"Sure," I told them, that I could do.

Having new voices on the team (and in my head) was refreshing, but Nora was still my coach. Under her watch, I swam roughly 30-35 kilometers per week, while working to perfect my new stroke. Most of my work was in the pool, though I did travel to Las Estacas some weekends for long, languid swims.

I also traveled to La Jolla, north of San Diego, California, twice for two separate eight-hour swims in the chilly Pacific Ocean. These would be my longest swims in the run up to Hawaii. The first was in January and I did another in February. Both times I swam at a pace of 3 km/h for a total of roughly 24 kilometers.

The good news was my shoulder had healed up. It felt great, plus I'd endured eight hours in the cold water twice (the water temperature was around 16°C), which gave me confidence, but my re-engineered stroke was still a mess. In fact, I'd never swum slower. Nora and Ricardo agreed that I should go back to the form I'd been swimming with my entire life. Perhaps it was too late to teach this old dog anything new.

Those La Jolla swims revealed something else too: that my focus was not where it needed to be. I was cold water training, thinking ahead to the Cook Strait and especially the North Channel, the coldest swim of all, before I'd even attempted the longest swim on the docket. Mostly because I still didn't know what awaited me in Hawaii. I didn't understand how heavy the currents can be in the middle of the Pacific. All I knew was that water temperatures in the Ka'iwi Channel in late March range between 23-26°C, which is very comfortable territory. Sure, the distance was a bit longer, but a swim in tropical waters sounded like a pleasure cruise compared to the dark, 12°C degree water between North Ireland and Scotland.

Not that I wasn't warned. In the weeks before leaving for Honolulu, I emailed my friend Forrest Nelson, one of the greatest open water swimmers ever. He'd swam the Ka'iwi Channel twice, once in each direction, so I asked him for some last-minute advice. Within two hours, he wrote back.

"I know you're a great swimmer," he wrote, "but you are in for a BIG one."

My team and I flew into Honolulu on March 18th. With me this time were my personal physician, Ariadna del Villar, her husband, Hugo, and their new baby, Joaquín. Nora was there too, of course. I wouldn't swim a channel without her. Brad Howe, my best friend from Stanford, is like a good luck charm, so I asked him to be there. Pablo, our photographer, decided to skip the trip and go to Cuba to document President Obama's speech and a Rolling Stones concert instead. Lucía and Ximena came along, however, not to crew for me on the swim, but to greet me when I finished.

We arrived in the evening, checked into our resort on Waikiki, and hit the beach to sink our toes in the white sand. It was warm outside, the air smelled sweet and I felt ready. Lucía asked me if I was nervous, but I wasn't. I'd done everything possible to prepare, and now it was time to perform.

The following morning Nora and I went for a two-kilometer swim before our meeting with the boat captain, Michael Twigg-Smith, and our kayakers, Jeff Kozlovich and Steve Haumschild, at the Waikiki Yacht Club. These men weren't the typical kayakers we'd meet before an ocean swim. They were among Hawaii's hardened outrigger paddlers. On each Hawaiian island, you'll find men and women who race outrigger canoes long distances, often between islands, and the most famous of those races is the one from Molokai to Oahu. These men knew the terrain as well as almost anyone else. Clearly I was in good hands, and after a glance at the weather report, we decided that on March 21st, my team and I would fly to Molokai to meet the captain and take our chances in the channel.

Hawaiians call the 45 kilometers of rough, wind-churned water that connects Oahu and Molokai the Ka'iwi Channel, or the Channel of Bones. Some think that's because the bones of fishermen and sailors who drowned in the tempestuous waters have washed up on both islands. Others maintain that it was named for Molokai's dry, volcanic landscape that may have reminded ancient Hawaiians of the Earth's exposed bones.

Though the Ka'iwi Channel has always been hazardous due to gale-force winds that can blow for days on end, and squalls that gather in an instant and can swamp a canoe in seconds, it's also long been a vital trade artery for Hawaiian communities for centuries. It's where fishermen have sought their daily catch for generations, and it's a testing ground where men and women, young and old, come to see if they have what it takes to get from island to island under their own power.

These days, the Ka'iwi Channel is probably best known for the the Molokai Hoe, the most prestigious ocean paddling race in the world. Aside from outriggers, there are divisions for stand up paddlers and prone paddlers—who lie face down on longboards and use their arms, and their board's glide, to propel them from beach to beach. Many of Hawaii's greatest watermen have attempted to paddle from Oahu to Molokai or vice versa, but precious few of those legends—and we are talking about some of the best lifeguards and surfers of all time—would try to swim the channel.

In 1939, William Pai reportedly became the first person to swim from 'Ilio Point on Molokai to Oahu's Sandy Beach. He was reported to have paddled a short distance offshore before jumping into the water to swim the rest of the way, so his feat wasn't certified. Keo Nakama completed the first certified swim from island to island in 1961. Altogether it's been done just 67 times by 63 different swimmers, who have all learned that there is a steep toll to be paid if you want to swim the channel in one go.

Landing on the rustic island of Molokai from Honolulu was like going back in time. Though the historic sugarcane plantations had been colonized by cornfields, Molokai still favored agriculture over tourism, and it was home to just 7,000 people. It was arid, not lush, its red earth offset by the deep blue Pacific Ocean.

We didn't plan to spend much time there. I arrived at noon, hoping for an immediate departure, but there were complications. A crushing shore break was pounding 'Ilio Point (which means "dog" in Hawaiian), the traditional starting point, and the big surf had sucked away all the sand. Because channel swimming rules demand a swimmer have all ten toes out of the water and on dry land on either end of the swim, I couldn't begin my swim there.

There was still a three-foot rock that I could have tried to climb up on and jump into the water from there, but given the rough conditions, that would have been foolish and dangerous. Thankfully, Captain Twigg-Smith had a work around. We boarded his boat, the *Stellina Mare* (Italian for Little Star of the Ocean) at Hale'o'lono harbor and sailed to La'au Point where we found a deserted beach, sheltered from the heavy swell. I knew starting from there would add another three kilometers to the swim, but I never question a captain. Plus, when you're already swimming a marathon, what's a couple more klicks?

I jumped from the boat and swam toward shore as Jeff settled his kayak into the water. His boat was fully loaded, ready to supply me with everything I needed. He waited for me beyond the foaming surf, while I waded ashore, caked in zinc from head to toe. The plan was for Jeff and Steve to rotate on two-hour shifts. When my toes were dry, I waded back into the ocean, ducked under the small waves and began to swim, ready and willing to contend with whatever the fates sent my way. They delivered a warning shot early on.

Fifteen minutes in, I felt my left armpit burn with pain that ricocheted through my body like shockwaves. I'd been stung by one of the channel's major hazards: jellyfish. It wasn't completely unexpected to encounter them, and after

10 minutes of excruciating pain, the sensation faded, and I was able to find an early rhythm.

For the first two hours, the current was with me and the water was warm and welcoming. I felt strong, and there were no jellyfish in sight. I'd done Tsugaru in under 13 hours, and figured, given the additional distance, it might take me 16 hours to finish Ka'iwi, 17 tops. My stroke was long and efficient, my shoulder felt great and thanks to the positive current, I was on pace to shatter my projected time. That is, until I hit the wall. This wasn't a wall of exhaustion. I wasn't even close to spent. This was the channel itself making its first stand. I'd swum beyond the shelter of Moloka'i, had entered the Ka'iwi Channel proper, and was met by a current that stopped me cold.

I swam in place for over an hour, without moving a single centimeter. Then there was the swell, which was so big that I couldn't track the kayak effectively. There were times I would only see them every third or fourth breath (instead of each breath), which messed with my head. There was little to no hope of tracking the support boat instead because, in that channel, the boat doesn't motor alongside you or just in front of you. The technique in Hawaii is for the support boat to buzz ahead about 100-150 meters and allow the swimmer to follow the kayak.

I was giving it everything I had and going nowhere, seeing nothing and nobody, as the minutes gathered into hours. I'd swam all over the world in countless rivers, lakes and channels. I thought I'd seen and felt almost everything a body of water can deliver, but I'd never set foot in Hawaii. I hadn't fully grasped how the island chain's remote location made it prone to severe currents and swells. I'd been so concerned about the North Channel that I hadn't done my homework, and now that I was confronted with the truth, I knew my friend Forrest was right, and that I was in for a long day and harrowing night.

That's when a humpback whale surfaced, 30 meters to my right. It was close to 15 meters long. Seabirds tailed it along the surface as it issued its powerful exhale, and another, before it ducked underwater, offering its fluke as if waving goodbye. Its presence relaxed me, and with the sun lowering to the west, the sky darkening, and the swell growing in size, I knew relaxation was my only choice—my only hope—given the conditions. The channel was trying to shut me down and I wasn't going to make it just by going hard. My job was to relax deeper, and tune into my form.

To remain focused and relaxed, I started to count my strokes from 1 to 100. Each arm movement was one stroke and when I hit 100, I started over again. The most important thing was that I was swimming pain free. That was a positive, plus with waves as big as these, I knew swallowing water wasn't going to be a problem. With smaller swells, taking in water is a real danger and drinking seawater on a channel swim can be a dehydrating disaster. It can make you nauseous and spur vomiting which only exacerbates dehydration. Rising and falling with a big swell, on the other hand, may feel disorienting, but it's not usually dangerous.

I made little progress in the next hour. A meter here, two meters there. The current was still fierce and fighting me with all its power, but I could feel a sense of forward motion and after two hours I finally began to move again. I swam on, counting my strokes, and clearing my mind.

Three hours passed like that, and I downed my Accel Gel and drinking water handed to me by my kayakers at the top and bottom of the hour, as usual. Then in hour six, I got hit again. Not by the current, but by a jellyfish bloom. These were Portuguese man o' war, among the most venomous marine life in the ocean. It was dark so I couldn't see how many there were, but I felt them graze my arms and legs, before one finally hit me dead on. Its tentacles lashed my face. It clung to the bridge of my nose and splayed out on both cheeks. I had no choice but to invite still more pain and pull it off with my bare hands.

The torture was excruciating. I gasped for air, my heart rate spiked, tears filled my goggles. It seemed the channel gods were throwing everything they could at me. Steve called to me as I treaded water. The crew on board the support boat directed their spotlight in my direction. They all wondered if I was okay. But when you're a long-distance swimmer, hurting is part of the deal. You must be able to separate yourself from pain whether it's saltwater ulcers in your mouth, chafing of your underarms or neck, or the venom of a man o' war. So I did what I always do. I waved them off, accepted my pain as taxes paid, and kept swimming.

When I stopped for my break ten and half hours into my swim, it was past midnight. The clouds had receded somewhat and the full moon played a game of hide and seek. Whenever the clouds cleared, if only for a few moments, moonlight danced on the surface. Jeff handed me my water bottle, as Nora peered down from the railing on the support boat.

"How far have we come?" I asked.

"We just passed the halfway point," Nora replied with a shrug. That was a gut punch, and she knew it. I was looking at a 20-hour swim at least. The longest I'd ever been in the water was my English Channel swim, which I completed in 18 hours and 19 minutes. I would soon be swimming into uncharted territory, with no guarantee of success, but I wasn't going to feel sorry for myself. What good would it do to play the victim, blame the conditions, the channel gods, the merciless jellyfish? That wasn't going to power me to Oahu. Instead, I thought about Gibraltar.

When I arrived in Spain and found out we would have to swim the very next morning, after 32 hours of travel, and very little sleep, I didn't dread it. I welcomed the challenge because I knew I would have to adapt to those kinds of unexpected frustrations to successfully swim the Oceans Seven. My injury was another test, and now, in order to cross the Ka'iwi Channel, I would have to swim a longer distance and spend more time in the ocean than I ever had before. But could I handle it? It was a fair question because after swimming for fifteen hours my neck was pink and raw from turning my head to my right to breathe. My back and left arm burned from over a dozen jellyfish stings, and the muscles in my neck hurt from lifting my head so many times to search for the kayak in the swell.

Then at the sixteen-hour mark, with the sun rising, I stopped for my feed in yet another jellyfish bloom. That was one problem. According to the forecast on Wind Guru, the wind was supposed to have died down, but it was still gusting. That was another issue, and the swell was still severe. I sucked down water and gel while being lashed by the furious jellies, and when I started swimming again, I was stung in my face one more time, just for good measure. Stunned, I lost my concentration, panicked and gulped seawater, but I could not afford to stop. Not for an instant because at that moment the current was against me, driven by the wind, and gaining in strength. For the next two solid hours, my kayakers barely had to paddle. The boat didn't move. I was swimming in quicksand and going nowhere. It was demoralizing.

Back on land, Ximena and Lucía were following my progress, or lack thereof, through a satellite GPS tracker on the support boat. They'd attempted to do the same thing in Japan, but had trouble finding Wi-Fi so they were mostly in the dark. This time, they thought the tracker was broken as the hours dragged on. I told them I'd arrive first thing in the morning, but sunrise came and went, and I wasn't even close to shore. They kept refreshing the page, but for those two hours I didn't appear to be moving because I wasn't. That made Lucía nervous, which made Ximena anxious. As the hours piled up, the more nervous and anxious they became.

I responded to the adverse conditions with the same old routine. I counted my strokes to 100 and kept my breaks as short as possible. Two hours later, I'd set a personal record for the longest swim of my career, and the current relented. I was making forward progress again but, at my pace, I was still five long hours away from finishing the swim.

For the first time, I thought about quitting. I could end the swim right then and tell the world that the conditions were horrible, and that I'd set a new personal best. No shame there, but that wasn't what I'd come to Hawaii for, so I banished that notion, along with the first 18 hours of swimming, from my mind. If I didn't finish, those 18 hours were all for nothing anyway, so there was no reason to dwell on them. They were already in the past. Instead, I pictured the final five hours like it was just another Saturday morning in Las Estacas. Swimming five hours in a row while fresh is quite a test of stamina in its own right, but it was something I'd proven countless times that I could handle easily.

With 6.5 kilometers to go, the wind picked up once more, and the waves tossed me from side to side, but Steve was able to find a pathway through the gales and with him paddling out front, I was able to push through and continue to make progress. I felt a sense of peace that had bubbled beneath the surface of my struggle from the onset of my swim. My relaxed mind and heart had carried me through, and now I finally, mercifully neared the end.

The last hour was the most enjoyable of the entire swim. With each breath I could see the lush cliffs of Oahu loom into view, and though I was in pain, exhausted and sleep deprived and had been in the water for almost a full day, I felt so good, I actually considered waiting another 40 minutes so I could say I swam for 24 hours straight. Then I saw Lucía and Ximena on the beach, staring into the ocean, searching for me, and I knew it was time to stake my claim.

Landing at Sandy Beach can be tricky because of the shallow rock reef and the jumble of boulders, studded with razor sharp shells, on either side of the sandy cove. Jeff had made that landing hundreds of times, so he jumped out of his kayak, put on a set of fins and guided me home. When my toes grazed the sand bar bottom, I stood up and waded through the shallows toward Lucía and Ximena who stood on the beach, shoulder to shoulder, beaming with pride and relief. With my toes dry, I raised my arms in triumph and gave them both a huge hug. It took a long time—23 hours and 18 minutes to be exact—and a hell of a lot of suffering, but I made it. My crew cheered from the boat beyond the waves. We waved back, and the three of us watched as they motored out to sea and disappeared around the point.

With my arms around the most important women in my life, we headed to the public restrooms, so I could take a shower and dress in the clothes they had brought for me. I asked Ximena to find me a beer from the tailgaters in the parking lot. All she had to do was tell them I'd just swam from Molokai and they handed over the coldest bottle in their cooler. Then something strange happened. While rinsing off I felt dizzy, so I sat down at a picnic table where Ximena found me. She handed me the beer and sat across from me.

"Are you okay?" she asked, concerned.

"I'm fine... I think... just light-headed," I said. Lucía was there too. She thought it was my blood sugar and headed to the nearby vending machines to buy me a soda, but as she walked away I crumpled to the ground, blacked out, and began convulsing. Ximena watched, helpless. She called out to Lucía, who came running, screaming in total panic.

"He's dying!" She yelled. "Help! Please help!"

An alert lifeguard sprinted over with a bottle of oxygen and radioed an ambulance. Unconscious, my face looked contorted in a way that convinced the lifeguard that I might be having a stroke, and his composure didn't exactly calm Lucía's nerves. She was beside herself, but Ximena proved calm during the crisis.

When the paramedics arrived, Ximena filled them in on what I'd just been through. They lifted me onto a stretcher and loaded me into the back of an ambulance, but they didn't think I'd had a stroke, and neither did Ariadna. When Ximena finally got a hold of her, she was angry with me because I hadn't done my typical post-swim protocol like I said I would. I'd been horizontal for nearly 24 hours. I should have laid on my back with my legs elevated for 20-30 minutes before trying to shower and change clothes, much less have a beer. It was a silly mistake.

When I woke up in the ambulance, the paramedics could tell I was lucid and out of harm's way. To their credit, they didn't insist that I go to the hospital. They let me take my time, lay there and sip my coke, while we waited for our taxi to arrive. When it finally did, they released me. It wasn't until we were in the cab on the way back to the resort that Ximena let go and started to sob.

I felt terrible. In a way, she and Lucía had experienced a dry run of their greatest fear. That one day I would push too hard and swim too long, and that it would cost me my life. After all, I was 57 years old, trying to pull off a world-class athletic achievement. To some, my quest sounded insane, but they'd always believed in me. With more challenges to come, I hoped I hadn't cracked their faith.

My collapse muted our celebration, and we drove back to Waikiki mostly in silence, but inside, I must confess, I was ecstatic. In the face of difficult conditions, my shoulder performed well, I was rock solid mentally, and our team was too. When we arrived at the resort, I went straight to my room to have a real shower and some much-needed room service, paramedics orders. I ordered a club sandwich, two beers and two tequilas, and savored the last Herradura on the lanai overlooking the Pacific Ocean.

I had just two swims left on the board, but they wouldn't be easy. To finish the Oceans Seven, I would have to embrace a level of discomfort I'd never felt before and learn to love something I'd long feared: cold water.

As unlikely as it

seemed when I

first got the job,

leading Conalep

was beyond

gratifying. It

was thrilling.

IO

Uncertainty

riving out to Metepec for my first day on the job, I was full of doubt. When I first received the news from the Minister of Education that I was President Zedillo's choice to lead the Colegio Nacional de Educación Profesional Técnica (Conalep), I cried. I felt like after doing everything I could to help win the election, my career had bottomed out and that I was circling the political drain. Then I started asking around about what Conalep was, and my mind shifted from feeling irrelevant to inadequate. I was suddenly responsible for 262 schools nationwide, staffed by 10,400 teachers who taught a quarter of a million students.

Conalep was one of the largest high-school systems in Mexico, and these were technical schools. Or at least they'd started out that way. They were meant to churn out qualified technicians. But in the nearly two decades since its inception

213

in 1978, it had morphed several times and become a complex educational morass that was hard to define, and frankly didn't have a great track record. I was tapped to be its savior.

On that long car ride, I was mired in uncertainty. I had no experience in education and was far from a technical school product. I had studied German and economics. Part of me wondered if I was being set up for failure. That was my fear talking, but at the same time I knew that even if that were true, my fate was not predetermined. With the right focus, even long odds can pay off. But where would I begin?

The best news I heard upon accepting the job was that Conalep was fully funded and that I would oversee my entire budget. As soon as I arrived through the glass doors and walked up to my second-floor office, I opened those books. There was a lot of room for improvement. Principals were being paid less at Conalep schools than at other systems of public education, and were trying to make up their lost income with "extracurricular" income. We had a top-heavy administrative staff that didn't have any direct impact on our students, and teachers were underpaid.

The more I looked into the numbers the more disconcerting stories I heard. Like how most of our principals were running cafeteria cartels. To make up for their low wages, they took money from cafeteria suppliers in exchange for a contract to sell food to our kids. They also made money by selling school supplies and charging for photocopies. I changed all of that straightaway. Principals got a significant wage increase but had no fiscal authority over the cafeteria or school supplies, and we updated the copiers across the system, so it became impossible for them to take a cut.

Over those first few weeks I made my rounds, visiting schools across the country. They all had a laundry list of problems. The entire system did, and without a background in education to fall back on, I did what I knew how to do, and that's bring to Mexico something that hadn't been available to us before.

When I was a kid that meant Speedo gear. At the Trade Ministry, it was a new standard of cleanliness for public restrooms in government buildings, getting top-of-the-line computer equipment for our offices, and bringing a fledgling computer network—engineered by Microsoft thanks to future billionaire Steve Ballmer (but paid for by Mexico)—to rural Mexico, which enabled us to better track harvests for commodities markets. Now it was time to uplift Conalep with a similar strategy, by applying modern, global standards to a stagnating Mexican institution.

My first stop on any school visit was always the principal's office. We'd shake hands, have coffee, and then begin meeting on our list of action items. In those early days, we were going over budgets and implementing testing standards, so we could assess our students', and our schools', strengths and weaknesses. All of that was expected, and the principals were prepared for it, but when the time came for me to use the bathroom, they were often caught off guard.

One nice thing about being a boss is you can get up during a meeting without having to explain yourself. Of course, like any concerned host, the principals would always ask where I was headed.

"I'm going to the bathroom," I'd say casually, and make my way toward the hall where the student restrooms were located.

"Oh, no, no, no," they'd respond, "use this one," and they'd point toward the faculty restroom or the private bathroom in their office. At which point I'd smile, shake my head, and stroll toward the student bathrooms anyway. I swear I heard a few of those principals gulp in terror, and almost all of them went ghost white. With good reason. This was their worst nightmare.

They all knew what their bathrooms looked like. Stalls were smashed, walls scrawled with graffiti, pipes clogged. There were no mirrors. I'm not describing a single bathroom in one school, or the worst-case scenario in a handful of schools. System-wide, our bathrooms were an embarrassing mess. I remembered my first big success under Serra was fixing the Trade Ministry's bathrooms and how improving something so basic improved pride among employees. My bet was the same thing could happen among our students.

Even more important was the effect it would have on our young women. Many of them would stay home when they were menstruating because the bathrooms were so disgusting, which meant they were missing class and falling behind every month. As a father of a young daughter that was unacceptable to me, so improving the bathrooms, adding mirrors, and upgrading the plumbing became a big focus in our first months on the job.

From there, I shifted to language and computer skills. Some schools had computers and others did not, and when I visited a school with a computer lab I'd never see kids using the machines. The computers were always shrouded in their plastic covers, wrapped up and protected from human hands.

"Why do the computers have condoms on them?" I deadpanned on one school visit, obviously annoyed.

"To protect them, Director General," the principal replied. "They are very expensive, and we don't want anything to happen to them." Protect them, he meant, from the students who were supposed to be using them.

I visited schools in Puebla, Chiapas, and Michoacán where cases of computer equipment hadn't even been opened. We'd delivered the hardware for up-to-the-minute computer labs, and, out of fear, the principals had failed to build them out. Most thought they were doing the right thing by protecting expensive equipment, but this was the mid-1990's, the first great tech boom was underway, and our technical schools had quarantined computer labs. It made no sense. Only a few students had access to the machines and they never had enough time with them to learn how to operate them, let alone program them. In my mind, all students needed access to computer labs that were open and available before and after class.

So, we installed functioning computer labs wired with dial up internet to empower our students with connectivity. I called my good friends at Microsoft to make sure all our terminals had Windows installed. Most top private schools in Mexico didn't have anything close to what we provided, and our kids were almost all from working class neighborhoods. But that's exactly what set my Conalep tenure apart from those of my predecessors. I wanted and expected my school system to be competitive with the very best schools in Mexico. Conalep may have been launched as a way to produce technicians for the domestic economy, but the schools I was in charge of would be connected to the wider world and provide a lens through which students could see all their infinite possibilities and dream bigger than they'd ever dared before.

Part of that came down to language. When I first arrived at the Conalep headquarters, I was one of the few on staff that spoke English. Almost none of the school principals or teachers knew English and obviously, students weren't learning it either. In a globalizing economy that was economic suicide, so I started requiring my gifted students to study English for three years.

I also pared down the curriculum. When I first arrived, our technical schools certified students in 132 careers. I couldn't even think of 132 careers if you gave me a week, so I spoke to my friends and colleagues in the private sector, education experts, and state governments across the country, and together we distilled a list of 29 vital and viable careers. They included the old Conalep standards—mechanics, electricians, accountants, hospitality and food and beverage professionals—but we added jobs better suited to the new technological age, including an updated telecommunication curriculum and a computer programming track. Whatever they studied, I required my students to play sports and study music and language, as well, so they could have a well-rounded experience and be inspired, and we invited business representatives to visit our campuses and interview graduating students, so they could fill vacant positions as soon as possible, and so our students could graduate with paying work waiting for them. Unfortunately, not everybody graduated. Far from it.

Despite all of our myriad improvements, we couldn't make a dent in the major dropout problem I'd inherited. On average, our students spent just three semesters in school.

We needed to give them something in those three semesters that would last a lifetime. Again, we turned to Microsoft and started a program that would eventually be named Microsoft Academy. It was a certification program for students to get hands-on training in Microsoft Office, something I hoped would help them in their career even if they slipped through the gaps in our system and had to build a life without a diploma.

I'd been part of an administration that had negotiated NAFTA, and brought a global economy to Mexico, and now my job was to create a workforce that met the demands of that economy. I wanted to teach the next generation of tech entrepreneurs and, blessed with my own budget and a massive staff, I could actually implement everything we dreamed up. As unlikely as it seemed when I first got the job, leading Conalep was beyond gratifying. It was thrilling.

Of course, there was the small matter of actually living in Metepec, a municipality of roughly 210,000 people, which I'd always considered the most boring place in the country. I obviously couldn't make the two-hour commute to and from my house twice a day, so I called on my friends at the Four Seasons Mexico City, which was set in Paseo de la Reforma, only 45 minutes from Metepec. The manager offered me a favorable rate, and the Four Seasons became my home away from home. It was good living, but it didn't last long.

A few weeks later, I was at an event with President Zedillo and his staff when I caught him staring at me from across the room with a severe look in his eye. When he saw me glance back, he walked over.

"Come here," he said, "I want to talk to you."

I followed him like one of my students who had just gotten busted by their principal. I knew I was in deep trouble but had no idea why.

"I've been told that you're living at the Four Seasons," he said. I nodded, contrite. He shook his head. "Okay, well you don't go back to that hotel. That is over." Then he walked away.

If you're wondering how it feels to disappoint a sitting president, I can tell you that it's not a lot of fun. To him, it didn't matter that the rate I negotiated at the Four Seasons wasn't exorbitant and fell within my budgetary requirements. We had just survived yet another devaluation, and appearances mattered to Zedillo. He was running a clean administration, and when a government official is shacking up at the Four Seasons, that doesn't look good. I should have known better.

The following night I checked into a third-rate Holiday Inn, in the fourth rate city that is Metepec. I dropped my baggage on the thin carpet, pulled open the shades, stared out over the bleak skyline, and resolved to spend as little time there as possible.

Weekends were easy. I would go back to the city or fly to Monterrey to see Lucía. We weren't yet married, but we were madly in love and headed in that direction. Midweek was another matter. Sure, I could visit schools, and schedule meetings in the city, but I had plenty of work at headquarters too. I couldn't avoid the place forever.

On my first morning living in Metepec, I was shaken from my dreams by a 4:30 a.m. wake up call. I sat on the edge of my bed, wiped my eyes, took a deep breath, and suited up to run 15 kilometers before work. Moderately depressed,

I strolled out the sliding glass doors of the Holiday Inn to the welcome surprise of seeing a blur of cyclists spin past. They were fully geared up in lycra, riding top of the line bikes up a winding road that led to the lip of a 4,500-meter volcano, the Nevado de Toluca.

It was January 1995, I was training for my first Ironman Triathlon in Kona, Hawaii, and it turned out that by dumb luck I'd been stationed in the Boulder, Colorado, of Mexico (Boulder is a mecca for triathletes in the States thanks to its most honored resident, Ironman legend Dave Scott). When I returned from my run, the hotel staff explained to me that athletes from all over the world based themselves in Metepec in order to train at altitude. I became one of them. My days always began with a swim followed by a long run or ride up the volcano. Ah, yes, Metepec. The training terrain was so good I actually grew to love the place.

But I still wanted to be a visible General Director. One of the criticisms of previous Conalep administrations was that the directors didn't travel to see the schools with their own eyes, meet the teachers and principals, and get to know the students and their parents. Early on, I told my staff that we needed to be accessible and that I would travel anywhere in the country as long as they could locate a pool for me to train every morning.

It was a beautiful thing to watch the transformation of the Conalep schools over the years. With clean bathrooms, vibrant computer labs and a streamlined curriculum, the buildings hummed with a new energy and efficiency, and our graduation rate went up by 6%, but I thought we could do better. And if I hadn't been so committed to visiting the schools and seeing them with my own eyes, I don't think I ever would have stumbled onto one of the main sources of our dropout problem: teenage pregnancy.

I started at Conalep seven years after a landmark 1988 study was coordinated by the National Population Council (Conapo), which illuminated the sexual tendencies of Mexicans, especially teenagers. It was called "National Survey on Sexuality and Family in Junior High School," and it rocked our society to its core. In a country where religion, primarily the Catholic church, plays such an imposing role, sex was a new discussion, and not entirely welcome. The survey touched upon adolescent sex and determined the average age when Mexicans lose their virginity was 16.5 years old. It found that 26% of all pregnancies were to parents under the age of 18, and it revealed startling statistics on homosexuality, and STDs, especially HIV.

Everything the study touched upon we saw in our schools, especially teen pregnancy, and when a girl got pregnant, it didn't just hijack her education. In many cases the teenage father dropped out too because he needed to go to work. That's how a cycle of poverty is created or perpetuated, and as far as my second in command, José Antonio Gómez, and I were concerned, Conalep had a responsibility to help curb teenage pregnancy by giving students the tools they needed to make better decisions. José and I agreed that we needed a robust sex education curriculum. That may sound basic to you, but in Mexico at that time, delivering sex education in a public school was considered revolutionary.

Miguel Limón, the Minister of Education—and my boss—was the first person I approached with our plan. Fausto

Alzati had resigned due to a falsified resume, and Miguel was appointed in his place before I ever set foot in Metepec. The two of us worked together during the Salinas administration and we were already good friends. In the days before I took over, Miguel summoned me to his office in Mexico City and delivered a strong message that stayed with me.

"I know you like politics," he said, "but if I ever find out that you are using Conalep for political reasons, you will be fired on the spot. You need to concentrate all of your efforts into fixing it and changing our students lives. They deserve nothing less."

Inspired, and with his support and a generous budget, I set out to do exactly that and built a track record of success. So, when I approached him with our newest and craziest idea yet, I was not at all surprised that he agreed immediately. For our children's sake, he knew it was time for us Mexicans to speak openly about sex.

Working in concert, Conalep and the Ministry of Public Education put together a new textbook for a course entitled *Sexual Education & Values*. The text addressed the basics of reproduction, obviously, but we also got into desire and didn't simply advocate abstention because we knew that wouldn't work. We discussed masturbation, contraception, and homosexuality. We were not going to say that there's only one way that you can have relationships. To us that was backward, inhumane, and a complete denial of reality.

Predictably, the delivery of those textbooks triggered an uproar from the Confederation of Employers of the Mexican Republic (Coparmex), a business organization with heavy influence on Conalep. Its board was stocked with old

223

money wealthy conservatives who didn't want teachers and counselors discussing sex with teenage students. Several other conservative organizations protested publicly, as well. We were accused of promoting homosexuality and promiscuity, when we were simply trying to be real with our students, so they could make smart, healthy choices for themselves.

Despite the backlash, Miguel never wavered in his support. "Find a way to beat them," he told me. So, I went to the Coparmex board meeting to present our text and the films we planned to show our students. I also explained why we were moving forward with the program, proving our case with hard data. In response, they threatened to run a smear campaign in newspapers across the country, attacking me personally and Conalep as a whole. These were the guys who owned the papers, so it was not an idle threat, but when the current gets tough in the ocean, you don't quit and climb into the boat. You push forward and fight like hell to cross the current, and that's what we did.

Our next move was to introduce parents to our curriculum. We held open houses and invited all parents of teenagers 15 and up. 75,000 of them came to our teach-ins during which we showed them our textbooks and films. Every parent who attended a teach-in signed a letter in support of the curriculum.

Coparmex again threatened to launch their smear campaign the following week. I dared them to do it and told them I would happily print the 75,000 letters signed in support of our program. In the end, we held a series of tense meetings with Coparmex leadership, while we tested our curriculum in 15 schools as part of a pilot program. After the pilot was completed, Coparmex grudgingly agreed to publicly support our initiative, and our curriculum was implemented at Conalep schools across the country. Soon after, our dropout rate plummeted to new lows.

But it wasn't about the statistics to me. After all, it's impossible to make a direct statistical link between sex education alone and our dropout rate. What made me proud was our commitment to empowering students to make better decisions. We fought to give them more control over their lives, and a sense of belonging no matter who they loved. It was one of the highlights of my education career.

By then I'd married Lucía, had connected with Nora Toledano, and switched my athletic focus, at least temporarily, from triathlons to open water swimming. Work couldn't have been going better, I was staring down the English Channel and life was beautiful.

The General Director of Conalep serves for two terms of four years each, and with Zedillo still in power (the president serves six years), I was appointed and easily confirmed for a second term in 1999. By that time, I was busy incorporating competency-based education into our schools.

There were a few models out there to emulate. England had employed competency-based education—in which students learn by studying real-world scenarios rather than theory or abstractions—since the 1970's, and it had spread throughout the Commonwealth. Canada had a great system, and so did Australia. We veered toward Australia because it was a country with an economy around the same size as Mexico's and they had a school system like Conalep in Technical and Further Education (TAFE). The TAFE leadership became our consultants.

Success does not usually come down to talent or luck, it's rooted in endurance and perseverance. It's about having enough faith and will to withstand discouragement and pain, and never give up.

One of the first things we did was evaluate and re-train our teachers. The teachers didn't love being evaluated, but we backed that up with a solid training program, and by the time the presidential race heated up again in 1999, we'd trained all 14,000 teachers in our system. Unfortunately, I wasn't allowed to see that project all the way through.

A little over a year after swimming the English Channel, I found myself out of a job. Vicente Fox, a conservative, won the 2000 election, defeating the PRI candidate, Francisco Labastida. It was an upset victory because after six years of Zedillo, during which the benefits of NAFTA really started to show, it seemed like the country would opt for the status quo. After all, disposable income was on the rise nationwide. Mexico City was booming with development, and we had more children in high school than ever before, but Fox captured the imagination of the country in a way our candidate could not.

I didn't participate in the PRI campaign this time. In fact, I was in Italy on election night and wasn't too concerned about our defeat (at least not personally) because I still had two more years left in my term. Then, not long after his victory, Fox's staff asked me to be a part of the Ministry of Education's transition team. If anything, I was optimistic about my future at Conalep. Within weeks, however, I was fired without cause and became just another 40-something, midcareer professional looking for work with no idea what I would do next. All I knew was it would not be in the public sector. I was done casting about waiting for appointments, subject to the whim of politicians or the general public. I'd been a businessman since I was a young kid, and I wanted to be in business again. But what would I do?

At first, I took some wrong turns. I started a consulting firm with my two ex bosses, Miguel Limón and Jaime Serra, but after running my own show for so long that felt like a step back, so I left the business and moved onto a new start-up geared toward creating efficiency in supply chains. It was a good business, but the founder and I ended up arguing and within a year I was out, losing my initial investment and all my stock.

In other words, my private sector reboot started with two failures, but Lucía didn't lose faith in me and I didn't panic because sports had prepared me for life. The discomfort that you feel when you do an Ironman, or attempt marathon swims across open channels, prepares you for those periods of psychic, emotional and even financial turmoil that are bound to come your way eventually.

When you push through extreme pain in the water, your discomfort is immediate and intense. All you want to do is quit, but if you persevere despite all that, you will become conditioned to endure even more discomfort the next time around, and that's the key to success. Success does not usually come down to talent or luck, it's rooted in endurance and perseverance. It's about having enough faith and will to withstand discouragement and pain, and never give up.

By then, I knew what it felt like to have a job. It was the easiest thing in the world. Paychecks come in on time, and life is relatively stable. Being your own boss, on the other hand, is like being flung out in the open ocean where you're subject to weather, currents, and bad luck. But no matter what comes at you, nothing outside of you predetermines your fate. Your success or failure in a given situation will almost always depend on how you respond to external conditions. No matter what I'm doing or how high the stakes, my response will never change.

I will always just keep swimming.

The North Channel loomed

large in my imagination,

and I needed to test myself

in the cold, which steals

the air from your lungs,

kicks you in the gut, and

colonizes your mind.

11

Catalina (Again) & Cook Strait

2017 was my cold-water year.

My original plan after completing the Ka'iwi Channel was to take on the North Channel the following August and, if all went well, finish my Oceans Seven push by swimming New Zealand's Cook Strait in the Southern summer (meaning February or March) of 2017. Even after I was recruited to join the PRI as the Secretary of Physical Activity and Sports, I saw no reason to divert from that schedule. I got my swims in because no matter where I was in Mexico, I always arranged to have access to a pool, even if that meant swimming at odd hours. As usual I swam 30-35 kilometers each week and on the weekends, I would swim for four hours at Las Estacas. I felt confident and strong of body and mind until I traveled to San Francisco in June of 2016.

San Francisco, one of my three favorite cities in the world, also happens to be blessed with one of the greatest open water swimming communities on the planet. At the center of it all are two iconic clubs—the South End Rowing Club and the Dolphin Club—set side by side, adjacent to the Hyde Street Pier, just down the street from Fisherman's Wharf. Their shared beach and bite-sized cove are known in San Francisco as Aquatic Park.

Ever since the clubs were founded in the 1870's, swimmers and paddlers have gathered there to swim or race vintage wooden row boats in the frigid, murky, foggy San Francisco Bay. Then they hit the saunas and down whiskey together to warm their icy bones.

The wood paneled halls of both clubs are lined with photos and plaques engraved with names of those who have accomplished the most famous channel crossings in the world. After strolling through them, gazing at the hardware, absorbing the history, and meeting the members of this secret society of adventurers—as my friend and fellow Oceans Seven swimmer, Kim Chambers, describes them— the world's toughest marathon swims start to feel attainable. And when new swimmers join the clubs and set a goal to swim, say, the English Channel, they are always encouraged to follow through, and are supported with training and fundraising advice.

Most serious Bay Area swimmers belong to one club or the other, though a few are members of both. I'm a member of the South End Rowing Club because they have fewer rules.

Swimmers from the Dolphin Club aren't tolerated to swim outside the confines of Aquatic Park—meaning beyond a roped off section of the bay. That's understandable given the heavy boat traffic and real concerns about fog and hypothermia. The warmest the San Francisco Bay gets is still a frigid 17°C. Most of the year the water temperature ranges from 9-14°C, which is exactly why I traveled to San Francisco in June of 2016. The North Channel loomed large in my imagination, and I needed to test myself.

But you can't really test yourself in a cordoned off cove that extends about 200 meters from shore. That's not open water swimming. It's glorified pool swimming. Sure, it's cold as hell, and swimming for long periods in that water while wearing only a Speedo, swim cap, and goggles is still challenging, but it's not the same thing as dealing with such temperatures while being tossed in the foreboding tides of the untamed San Francisco Bay.

233

So, my friend and escort kayaker Miguel Meléndez and I suited up for a four-hour swim to the foot of the Bay Bridge and back. The water temperature that morning was around 14°C. When you wade into water that frigid without a wetsuit, the only thing you can do to acclimate is to start swimming immediately, which is hard with the cold stealing the air from your lungs, kicking you in the gut, and colonizing your mind. Not to mention that vicious brain freeze headache that blooms the second you go face down.

The pain can be excruciating, but usually lasts just the first ten minutes of any cold-water swim before receding to the back of your mind. After that, the headache fades and your blood flows to your core, which creates a numb membrane on the surface of your skin. It's tempting to get comfortable in that membrane, because you do feel warmer, almost energized, but the second you stop swimming to have a look at, say, the Golden Gate Bridge illuminated by the rising sun, the cold comes thundering back and punishes you anew.

By the time we entered the water on that June morning, with a thick blanket of white fog threading through the skyscrapers of downtown San Francisco, I hadn't swum in temperatures below 16°C for more than an hour in years. I had been training in La Jolla, but the Pacific Ocean seldom gets below 16°C that far south in California, where our warm Mexican waters mingle with brisk Alaskan currents.

I loved being in the middle of the bay, in a city that was truly my second home. I enjoyed views of two iconic bridges and Alcatraz, and counted the massive container ships and steaming tug boats as they cruised in from the Pacific. But I wasn't seasoned, and after nearly an hour of feeling strong and capable, my confidence crumbled as the cold nibbled at my synapses, eroded that protective membrane, and seeped into my bones. There was no way I could make it all the way to the bridge and back. I told Miguel as much, through chattering teeth and ice blue lips, and we returned early. By the time we staggered ashore at Aquatic Park, we'd been in the San Francisco Bay for just over three hours. I was a shivering mess, so we didn't linger outside. We went straight for the sauna, where sitting in the dry heat, on the cedar bench, my mind ran on a loop.

If I couldn't last even four hours in temperatures like those that awaited me off North Ireland, how would I be able to swim over 12 hours in the North Channel? That swim was just two months away, and it was obvious I wasn't ready. Not only that: I was afraid, and not just of the cold. After all the effort, time, and money spent, I was afraid I couldn't achieve what I'd set out to do.

I was afraid of failure.

Back at the hotel, I called my team with the news. We would postpone the swim. At first, they were concerned I'd re-injured my shoulder, but once I explained it to them, Rafa and Ricardo understood. Nora wasn't happy. It's incredibly hard to book support boats for channel crossings. Many channels have a two-to-three-year wait list, and if we pushed it until 2017, she was concerned that I wouldn't be able to find a boat until 2019. She knew I wanted to be the seventh swimmer to achieve the Oceans Seven, and I was on schedule to achieve that, but Rohan More from India, Ion Lazarenco-Tiron from Moldova, and Steven Junk from Australia were lurking out there with the same goal, and if I was shut out of the North Channel in 2017, she said, any one of them might get there first.

Those were fair points, but if I tried to swim the North Channel in 2016, failure was guaranteed, and I would still have to book another trip in 2017, so why take the chance? Instead, Rafa, Ricardo and I made monthly pilgrimages to San Francisco, spending almost all our time at the South End Rowing Club and in the San Francisco Bay. By November, I was able to make the full Bay Bridge swim with Kim Chambers, who in 2014 had become the sixth person to swim the Oceans Seven. Kim is a dear friend, but on that particular swim she annoyed the shit out of me because the swim was so easy for her, and she wouldn't stop talking, while I was just trying to survive. Still, it did feel good to tap the concrete pylon of the Bay Bridge, fight the current all the way back to Aquatic Park and get out of the water without feeling terribly cold. It was a sign that I was getting closer to where I needed to be.

In physiological terms I was building more brown fat—a fatty layer embedded with capillaries surrounding the internal organs. That's what keeps newborn babies cozy in this cold world and enables hibernating mammals to stay warm while dreaming winter away. It's like an internal heating pad, but most people don't have it once they shed their baby fat. Open water swimmers need it to withstand the cold sea for half a day without becoming hypothermic, and you can only build brown fat by spending time in cold water.

My next scheduled Oceans Seven swim was the Cook Strait, between the North and South Islands of New Zealand in March. Although the water there would be far colder than in Hawaii, it wouldn't be a fair test of my abilities to deal with the type of cold I'd confront in the North Channel. This got me thinking about my friend Dan Simonelli's amazing Catalina Channel swim on January 15th, 2016. He had done it to celebrate the 89th anniversary of George Young's maiden crossing, but also to prepare for his own English Channel crossing later that summer. In all the many years since Wrigley's race, Dan was just the third to successfully swim the complete distance in the month of January.

I called him the following November and was left with the painful revelation that a successful January crossing of my own would give me some experience to lean on when things became difficult in the middle of the North Channel. If I could pull it off.

According to Dan, one of the most difficult aspects of a Catalina swim in January was organizing it. The Catalina Channel Swimming Federation doesn't open its swim season until April each year, and in order to persuade the Federation's board to allow his attempt, he had to make his case in writing, supported by a recent medical evaluation. I followed the same protocol and in early December, my attempt was approved. On the 90th anniversary of George Young's incredible feat I would try to become just the fourth swimmer in history to cross the Catalina Channel in January.

When I told Nora and Rafa, they were both pissed. Rafa was concerned that it would be too close to the Cook Strait attempt, and that I wouldn't have enough time to recover. As a great athlete herself, Nora is a creature of habit and lives by plans made as if they were frozen in shatter-proof bronze. Here I was changing that plan, again, which would alter our training and tapering schedule. They didn't like it, but I'd made up my mind.

Swimming for four hours in the San Francisco Bay is a challenge, but the North Channel would require a swim of more than 12 hours. That's a significant difference. I needed to know if I had the stuff to get it done. I'm not talking about building more brown fat. This swim would be about mental strength and nothing else.

Days before my Catalina swim, Lucía, Ximena, David, and his girlfriend (now wife) Itzi traveled with me to San Francisco for New Year's Eve. We had a big party, of course, and the next morning, I woke up a bit after sunrise and went to the club for a New Year's Day swim in Aquatic Park. The water was just 10°C, nearly as cold as the Bay gets, but this time I was swimming within the boundaries, to the flags at the mouth of the cove. Nevertheless, the cold was so bad, my head pounded like never before. Ten minutes passed. Then fifteen and twenty, but I still couldn't catch my breath. Dizzy with fear and cold-water shock, I panicked, and swam toward the pier, where I climbed out and fell to my knees, shivering, with my head in my hands. My skin was ghost white, my lips blue, my bones rattled so hard that I was a living, breathing New Years noisemaker, and I'd only been in the water for 42 minutes.

My friend Simon Dominguez, the president of the South End Rowing Club, found me there. Simon is a great swimmer, and a beast in cold water. He once swam the length of Lake Tahoe, a high-altitude alpine lake that stretches 35.5 kilometers from end to end. He had also made a valiant and unprecedented attempt to swim 46 kilometers from the Golden Gate Bridge to the Farallon Islands, but with just five kilometers to go, and with his neck chafed and bleeding, the local great whites took a close interest in him (there are a lot of them around the Farallones). So, he was pulled from the water as a precaution.

Simon didn't know how far, or rather how little I'd actually swum that morning. He asked me the basic questions (my wife's name, my hometown, and the day's date) to gauge whether or not I was hypothermic. Then he helped me up and led me inside to that familiar cedar bench in the sauna where I crawled back into my own head. I'd been training in cold water for seven months, but after that miserable performance, I had to wonder if it had been enough. I'd soon find out. My Catalina swim was just two weeks away.

My team and I boarded my support boat in Long Beach Harbor at 7:00 p.m. on January 15th. Forrest Nelson, the current president of the Catalina Channel Swimming Federation, and Carol Sing, the Federation's secretary, stopped by to wish me luck. Dan Simonelli had agreed to be one of my kayakers and was on deck organizing supplies near Tom Hecker, another world class open water swimmer and the Federation's official observer for the crossing. Add Nora and I, and we had four Triple Crowners and four members of the International Marathon Swimming Hall of Fame on one boat. It was a great feeling to see so many wonderful swimmers take an interest in my attempt, on the 90th anniversary of the maiden Catalina Channel swim. I wanted to make them, and the late George Young, proud.

In the hours before any crossing, there is no place in my mind for anything other than success. I forget unresolved issues in my professional life, I check out from the travails of Mexico and our troubled world, and I sign off from dwelling on any lingering personal problems. My 100% focus is on my plan for the swim itself and the ocean before me. Yet, with all those great athletes surrounding me, I was a little bit nervous because I had a lot riding on the outcome. Most significantly, I needed to last at least six hours in sub-16°C waters to qualify for the North Channel in 2017. I also wanted to equal Dan's feat, and needed this success to tackle the North Channel with confidence.

While Pablo snapped photos, Ariadna set up her medical supplies and Miguel Meléndez, my other kayaker, helped organize the feedings, Forrest took me aside.

"It's cold out there," he said with an arched eyebrow, gesturing toward the water.

"I've been in colder," I said. He nodded. We both knew that crossing the entire channel, in water temperatures below 16°C at night and in just a Speedo, swim cap, and goggles, would demand a monumental effort and bring a lot of pain.

"Look, Antonio, I know what you're capable of and that you know how to control the pain and endure some extreme conditions," Forrest said, "but we don't always get to decide how things go and... if we push too hard... sometimes..." He couldn't find the words to finish his thought. Instead, he placed his left hand on my shoulder and extended his right. "Just be smart, okay?"

We shook on it.

The trip to the island from Long Beach Harbor went by in a blink. The wind was up and there was a fair bit of swell, but the boat powered right through it. In under an hour, we bobbed in front of Long Point. Miguel Meléndez and Dan Simonelli suited up and loaded the kayaks, Rafa warmed me up and stretched me out, and Nora swathed my skin in zinc oxide and Vaseline. I was about to jump in and swim to my starting point, when a dolphin breached the surface then leapt into the night, exposed from nose to tail, before disappearing into the black water.

"It's 14°C!" shouted René Martínez, Itzi's brother-in-law who would swim Catalina later in the year. He'd just checked the boat's thermometer at Nora's request. It was a bit colder than we'd anticipated, but it was too late to whine about it. There was work to do.

Nora approached me with her iPhone. "Would you like to check Wind Guru one last time?" She asked. I shook her off. I already knew that winds were forecast to be strong all night, and it was time to see how I'd perform in adverse conditions one more time. I stepped to the edge of the deck and jumped in.

Swimming to the island, I could feel the cold in my gut, but not in my head. This meant that the water temperature wasn't as severe as in San Francisco Bay. On the beach, toes dry, I gave the signal and started the 32.3-kilometer swim back toward the California mainland.

High winds had cleared the sky. The air was brisk, the moon nearly full, but the chop, which was close to two meters high, was more than any swimmer would hope for. Before leaving the hotel, I had a bowl of tomato soup, and on the trip out from the mainland I'd eaten a muffin. None of that settled in my stomach. Tossed in the cold seas, I got sick, and vomited over and over again. I had no choice but to swim on.

By the fifth hour, my left arm hurt, and alarm bells were ringing in my head. The pain reminded me of what I dealt with in the Tsugaru Strait. An injury on an arguably unnecessary swim just two months before swimming the Cook Strait, my second-to-last channel in the Oceans Seven, was the absolute worst-case scenario. At the bottom of the hour, I swam over to the boat and asked Rafa and Ricardo what could be done to alleviate the pain.

Their concern was obvious, but they weren't permitted to touch me and stopping at that moment didn't make much sense either. I needed at least six hours to qualify for the North Channel. They discussed it and told me to focus on swimming from my core, extending my arms out from my abdomen, twisting my hips, and relying less on my shoulders to pull myself across the water. I executed their suggestions and my arm felt better, but soon my groin started to throb.

After that, further conversations with my team became pointless. Thanks to stiff winds, we couldn't hear each other, so I stopped even trying. Occasionally, they wrote messages for me on their white boards, but if I spoke to anybody at all it was Dan or Miguel, depending upon which of them was on duty. Miguel couldn't hack the 16-knot winds or the heavy seas for long. Halfway through, he'd become too seasick to paddle. It would be up to Dan to see me through.

The big moment on any Catalina swim is the energy transfusion that blesses the swimmer at dawn. All night long, the sky was cloudless. With so much wind, I was sure it would stay that way and that sunrise would bring the warmth and energy I so desperately needed. Indeed, at first the sunlight was so intense, I opted to switch out my goggles for a tinted lens, but after eight hours of swimming, my hands were too cold to feel, much less bend my fingers. It took intense concentration to pry my goggles off my head and replace them.

As if on cue, with my new goggles in place, the wind brought rain clouds that blotted the sun. The temperature dropped again and after a short respite from the wind in the pre-dawn light, whitecaps bloomed all around me. The forecast predicted more of the same for the next several hours, but there was some good news too. Aside from my fingertips, my body was holding up well. I wasn't shivering, my stomach had settled, and I made good progress until I hit an unforgiving wall.

With the shore visible in the near distance, I was held in place by a negative current. We were 13 hours into the swim and Ariadna watched the clock, worried about hypothermia. But I wasn't coming to the support boat for my feeds, so she couldn't examine me properly. Dan was the one watching my back and being an experienced open water swimmer himself, he wasn't the type to pull me from the water out of fear. He would have to be 100% sure that I was in distress before he made that call. Though I was slowing down thanks to the unfavorable current, I showed him just enough to maintain his confidence.

It was a long swim, and the cold took its toll. By the time I staggered to the rocky Palos Verdes shore around noon on January 15th, I'd been in the water for 14 hours and 27 minutes. I was shivering so badly that I could barely stand up straight. My bones rattled, my skin was ghost white, and my eyes were almost swollen shut.

I wobbled on the beach, raised my arms high, and when the horn sounded, I crawled back toward the water and let Dan lead me toward the boat, which idled beyond the surf. I had just enough strength in my arms to climb the boat's ladder, and as soon as I reached the deck, Ricardo and Rafa took me by the shoulders and sat me in a chair. Ariadna checked my eyes with her flashlight and the three of them led me to a shower on the boat where sea water, warmed from the boat's engines, washed over me. When someone is hypothermic, the water you use to warm them up can't be piping hot. This shower was lukewarm, but I was so cold, it felt like a cascading hot spring.

Ariadna monitored my vital signs, wrapped me in fleece and a foil space blanket, and pressed heat packs against my skin. It was too soon to tell how much strength my January crossing had sucked from my bones or how long it would take to recover. All I knew was that I had become the fourth person to make the Catalina crossing in January, I had officially qualified for the North Channel, and that if I still had breath in my lungs by March, Cook Strait was next.

Our flight to New Zealand nine weeks later took 29 hours from start to finish. It routed through San Francisco, but this time, with my entire team in tow—Ariadna and her one-year-old son Joaquín, Nora, Rafa, Ricardo, Pablo, and Lucía—we didn't enjoy the city or swim in the Bay. Instead, we had a three-hour layover before a trans-Pacific flight that night. While we waited, I started to get the chills. My throat was sore, and my sinuses were clogged. Ariadna gave me antibiotics, but things got worse on the plane; not the ideal overture to any adventure.

Wellington, New Zealand, is a gleaming city set among lush green hills, which spills onto a placid sapphire blue bay at the southern tip of New Zealand's North Island. Despite the beauty, I felt awful and hadn't felt anywhere close to my top fitness level since my Catalina swim. My muscles had been achy and tired, and while I'd been putting in the kilometers, I was concerned that Rafa and Nora had been correct all along. Catalina had been a big risk and it remained to be seen if it would torpedo my Cook Strait swim and throw off the rest of my year.

We stayed at the Intercontinental, one of Wellington's finest hotels, and were pleasantly surprised to meet a Mexican woman from Guanajuato clerking the check-in desk. Before NAFTA, it would have been extremely rare to meet a young person from a relatively small Mexican city working and studying in the capitol of a faraway country like New Zealand. But, in my opinion, that's what NAFTA brought to Mexico. It raised up our collective self-esteem. Overnight, we were no longer a Third World country on the periphery of prosperity. We were stakeholders in a global system, and over 20 years later, our children now study all over the world. Meeting her was another reminder that what we did under Salinas and Zedillo was truly important, but that didn't change the fact that I was an achy, coughing mess with less than a week to recover.

We met with our boat captain, Philip Rush, the next day. We'd been in communication for months but had never met face to face, and he wanted to see me swim. Philip wasn't the typical boat captain. For one thing, his boat was a barebones, 40-foot-long rigid inflatable (RIB). Also, while most boat captains aren't swimmers, Philip was a legend. He had two double crossings of the Cook Strait, a total distance of about 46 kilometers, on his resume, and he'd also swam non-stop across the English Channel three times in one go. When a swimmer with those credentials takes an interest in your form, you want to show your best stuff, but I was too sick to oblige. Instead, we found a warm place to relax and talk on a foggy morning. He came with both good and bad news. For most of my weather window, the forecast was horrible, but on the very first day, which was just five days away, the weather was supposed to be clear and mild, with superb conditions for swimming. He also mentioned that he had a perfect record piloting swims across the Strait in the 2017 season, which was obviously reassuring.

Two days later, on March 15th, I felt loads better and began a regiment of short taper swims, topping out at one hour a piece. My pace was strong, and though the water was a chilly 15°C, I was prepared for it. I'd trained hard in San Francisco and had proven myself in the Catalina Channel. My brown fat was well brined and ready to keep me warm on the 23-kilometer swim.

Cook Strait, known to New Zealand's original inhabitants, the Maori People, as Te Moana-o-Raukawa, connects the Tasman Sea to the South Pacific Ocean, and separates the country's two main islands. Swimming across brings its fair share of hazards. For one thing, it is similar in temperature to the Catalina Channel, but it's the fierce tidal flow, which can hold a swimmer hostage for up to eight hours, that can turn any promising start into total failure.

Although it's named for Captain James Cook, the English explorer who led the first European circumnavigation of present day New Zealand, Maori legend has it that it was Kupe, a legendary Polynesian navigator, who launched a sailing canoe from Tahiti and, guided by the stars, became the first to cross the channel and touch its shores. In the 19th century, whalers sailed in from Europe, and Wellington became the first European stronghold in what would soon become New Zealand.

Like the history of the channel itself, there are two versions as to who was the first to swim between the islands. Oral Maori history has at least one swimmer making the crossing as early as 1831. Some believe she was a woman who was escorted by a dolphin. I like to believe that's true. But for those of us dressed by Speedo, the first person to swim the strait was a man named Barrie Davenport in 1962. 13 years later, the great Lynne Cox became the first woman to officially cross.

Cook Strait is better thought of as a meniscus, where two powerful oceans converge, and like any crossing, a swimmer's schedule is weather dependent. Captains look for weather windows and monitor the tidal flow because the currents in Cook Strait fluctuate so radically, running hard in one direction for six to eight hours before reversing course and thundering in the other. And yet, knowing all of that, when we arrived at the harbor at 6:00 a.m. to meet Philip Rush, my mind was everywhere except on the task at hand. For one thing, Ariadna's husband couldn't make the trip, so that meant her son, Joaquín, would have to stay with Lucía in Wellington, and Lucía was anxious about caring for a baby who was going to be without his mother for the very first time. Pablo had just bought a drone and was so preoccupied with learning to fly it, and concerned it would be a huge failure, that he was stressing all of us out and asking Ricardo to help him manage it. Rafa, meanwhile, just had back surgery so he couldn't be on the boat with us. He was stuck in Wellington. It was a circus, but, when Philip arrived, he brought news that should have drowned out all that meaningless noise. The sublime weather he'd hoped for wasn't going to last as long as he originally thought.

"Today we will have about four to five hours of good weather, then the winds will begin to blow," he said. "We are expecting a strong storm and, if the conditions are not suitable, I will have to take the swimmer out of the water. No matter what. I have the last word."

His message could not be clearer and should have scared me straight, yet once I started out from the North Island at 7:30 a.m., I remained overconfident. The water was a manageable 15.6°C, the surface was clean, and I made the mistake of thinking that Philip was worried for no reason, and that it was going to be an easy day.

For the first five hours, the boat motored alongside my right side, but when the winds kicked up and the waves began to crest and foam, he moved to my left to block the havoc. Problem was, I don't breathe on my left and wasn't going to start on the sixth of my seven Oceans Seven swims. With no boat on my right to guide me, I didn't know where to look or how to track my path. During a rest break, Philip pointed to a mountain rising from the South Island coast.

"Just aim toward that mountain," he said. I did as he asked, but the wind got so bad, it kept pushing me off course. At times I was swimming so hard to my right I was almost parallel to the island. It didn't feel as if I was swimming to South Island at all, but out toward an open horizon. Tides from the Pacific drew me east, away from the destination of my dreams, and I knew that if I missed my landing point, I'd have to swim a lot more than 23 kilometers to make it across the channel. There was no place else to land for another 16 kilometers.

After swimming seven hours, I was on pace for a twelve-hour swim, a disappointing time to say the least, but I'd once swam nearly 24 hours, so it was still doable. It was just a matter of remaining in range of our landing spot and getting there before this storm grew even angrier. In the eighth hour, as I turned to breathe, my left hand landed on a jellyfish, floating translucent on the surface of a purple sea. Its venom pulsed through me, my eyes watered in my goggles, and I cursed my fate, but I did not stop.

However, my arms were churning at rate below 60 strokes per minute, which was slow for me, dangerously slow, and in the twelfth hour, I could see the landmark I'd been aiming for moving to my far left. I was losing touch with my destination and had to switch direction on the fly just as the wind picked up. Dark clouds gathered in force, and Philip told Nora I needed to pick up my pace to over 61 strokes per minute or we wouldn't beat the storm. She gave me the news, while the captain approached Pablo and Ricardo.

"Things don't look good," he told them, "These winds are going to get a lot worse very soon. We might have to get him out." They nodded, grimly, but kept the bad news to themselves.

"You have just two kilometers to go," Philip yelled in my direction a half hour later. It was the most optimistic and enthusiastic he'd sounded since the first hour. I nodded and decided not to accept any more feedings. It was time for the finishing kick. I picked up my pace and felt myself carving the water with ease. It was the best I'd felt since the very beginning of the crossing. Again, I heard Philip's joyful cry, "You're 800 meters away!" I looked up.

"Where should I go?" I shouted back. There were two mounds sticking up from the sea crowded with ruffled seagulls. It was the beginning of the South Island landmass, but there wasn't much of a beach.

"Swim to the left mound!" Philip yelled.

I made the distance as the first raindrops fell, and with just a few meters to go, I slowed down to time the swell. I was worried the rocks would be covered in sharp shells, but when the surf lifted me onto a pile of boulders, they were cushioned with sponges and seaweed. It was a forgiving finish to a difficult swim. Cook isn't a toes dry channel, so I leaned on the rocks awkwardly, with my feet still in the shallows, and raised six fingers toward the sky. Pablo's drone captured the moment. I'd done it. Six of seven channels were in the books.

Philip hammered the throttle as we raced the rain back to town, and after a beautiful dinner overlooking the channel, and one more night in Wellington, most of my team left for Mexico. Lucía, Pablo, and I went onto Queenstown.

In such an exquisite country, Queenstown is arguably the most beautiful city of all. Surrounded by jagged glacial peaks, it's the adventure sports capital of New Zealand, but on our second day there, Lucía slipped on the street, fell and hit her head on the curb. It was a terrible fall that came out of nowhere. We rushed her to the emergency room, where she was diagnosed with a concussion. The doctor said if she'd hit the ground any harder she could have died.

His words shook me, and while I waited in the ER, I couldn't help but dwell on how quickly things can change in this fragile world. In this life, there isn't time to relax, even after a victory. Certainly not if we are chasing our dreams, working to stake a claim and make our name. Those of us filled with ambition must keep that pedal mashed down because we never know when the show will end.

Once Lucía was discharged, we headed home to Mexico and my monthly pilgrimages to the San Francisco Bay continued. For the next five months, I would swim in the cold water, for hours upon hours, at every opportunity. I hoped to inoculate myself, to become immune to the cold, but part of me knew that was pure fantasy. When it comes to hypothermia, there is no pill you can take or vaccine you can ask for. Withstanding inhuman temperatures for hours on end is about learning to stave off panic by managing the mind with a combination of intense focus and deep relaxation. It's a skill of its own. I knew someone in Mexico City who could help me find that balance and prepare me for the greatest challenge of my swimming life. He'd been helping me on and off for over 20 years.

It was time to get back in touch.

"You will swim,

count your strokes,

keep your mind

blank, and focus on

your red pearl. That

will be your internal

thermostat."

12

Manage the Mind

Ever since Felipe Muñoz's magnificent swim on that magical day in 1968, sports have been my guiding light, and once I started training and competing in the pool myself, it became my rock, the one solid thing I could count on no matter what. Whether the fates have been kind or unfair, the tide low or high, my athletic pursuits have functioned as a bubble, a parallel life, a cocoon I can drop into to shut off all the noise of daily life and stay in the moment.

Often, that means pushing myself to the point of suffering, and suffering *is* the point. When you test yourself athletically, you find out who you are at your core. Are you willing to quit when things get difficult or do you have what it takes to push through? For most people, including me, that answer may change depending upon the day, which is exactly why sports are so powerful. They offer the opportunity to face difficulty, and even invite it, so that we can see what we're made of, day after day, week after week, year after year.

I'd had my share of successes and had failed on the big stage too, but the important thing is I always put myself back in the arena. And by testing myself, over and over again, from childhood to middle age, I had developed a self-confidence and toughness that can only come from managing the mind in extremely stressful, physical situations. Still, facing the North Channel, and almost certain hypothermia, was the most daunting of all the obstacles I'd ever faced. The cold ocean doesn't care who you are or where you came from, what you've done or plan to do. Human beings are not meant to swim 35 kilometers across a channel from North Ireland to Scotland, period. We aren't designed to endure water temperatures that hover around 13°C in the summer for more than half a day, without so much as a wetsuit to keep us warm.

That's what stood between me and the fulfillment of my dream, a dream I'd spent years pursuing. If I failed to cross this last channel, it would have all been a tremendous waste of time and energy. Yes, there would be lessons learned from this adventure, no matter the outcome, but coming so close and not getting there would be heartbreaking, so I resolved to do everything in my power to find success. That meant tuning into my deepest fears and learning how to better manage doubt, so I could push my limits. It meant calling Jaime Delgado and asking for help.

Jaime Delgado grew up hampered by a joint problem that prevented him from running and playing with the other kids in grade school. He kept trying, but his lack of dexterity made him an outcast as a teenager and ravaged his self-confidence. When he turned 17, however, he discovered karate. On his first day in the dojo, he was the worst in the entire group. The calisthenics and deep stretches were painful for him, because his joints and muscles were so stiff, but he persevered. He started off training for two hours a day before ramping it up to four, six, then eight hours each day.

The young man was so obsessed, he cut his hair like his idols, Bruce Lee and David Carradine, and within three years he earned a black belt. But karate was only the beginning. He went on to study tae kwon do, kendo, judo, and ninjutsu. He became a sensei, and when he was still just 21 years old, he was hired as Self-Defense and Physical Conditioning Coordinator by the Mexican police academy, where he trained officers in hand to hand combat.

Within four years, he had learned how to destroy someone's physical body 200 different ways. He could break bones, dislocate joints, bruise organs. He knew how to take a rolled-up newspaper and turn it into an effective weapon against opponents armed with knives. He knew how to kill, but in martial arts, it's all about balance and his next mission would be learning how to heal.

One day he heard that Chi Shian Ming, a kung fu and qi gong master from the Shaolin temple in China, was touring Mexico and giving seminars. The Shaolin lineage is revered across the martial arts because it goes beyond physical power, using energy and mental strength to heal and endure. Chi Shian Ming demonstrated his qi gong mastery, and Jaime was so impressed that he followed him to China, where he kept learning techniques to manage his body, mind, and energy.

After that he traveled to Tibet on his own and lived in the Drepung and Shiar Tse monasteries. It was during his time there that he learned of a mental technique Tibetan messengers used to endure low temperatures while running through the Himalayas for hours, from one monastery to another. The messengers taught him how to run with a relaxed focus and minimal energy expenditure. Running in this meditative state helped them keep warm, energized and pain free on a harrowing and demanding journey in the harshest of climates. They said it felt as if they were floating.

In the late 1980's, Jaime began working with athletes to help them develop mental strength, manage pressure, and overcome injuries. By the time I met him, he'd coached Davis Cup tennis players, soccer stars for Barcelona and Atlético de Madrid, Formula Renault drivers, professional golfers, and ultra marathoners. Yet the first time I heard his name was when he called me in 1998. He'd heard from Alex Kormanovski, a biochemist who used to study the effects of my training on my blood chemistry, that I was trying to swim the English Channel and he thought he could help. He didn't want money. He was so taken by the idea of helping someone capable of swimming long distances across open water that he offered to help me for free.

CHAPTER TWELVE

"Every athlete I work with claims their sport is the hardest one," he told me. "The soccer player says it is the only sport played with your feet. The horseman says they depend on an irrational animal. The tennis player says no ball comes at him the same. The golfer says it's the hardest because of the techniques and mechanics, and ultra marathoners must maintain their energy while running superhuman distances. But I can assure you that the hardest of all is what you are doing in open water.

"You must handle dynamic water temperatures and currents, contend with jellyfish and sharks and the permanent feeling of frustration of being completely dependent on nature. Not to mention do it all yourself from beginning to end."

He confessed that the innovations he hoped to share with me weren't new. Anything but. He wanted to demystify ancient martial arts and meditation techniques that he learned from his own masters and monks in the monasteries in order to help me not only persevere in the water, but excel. It was an easy yes. Very few people understand the commitment and difficulties that come with marathon swimming. It felt good to have his immediate support. Plus, I never make the mistake of thinking I have all the answers. I take all the help I can get. I went to meet him before dawn the following morning, and I have been in touch with him ever since.

The closer I got to the North Channel, the more I relied on him. Each Friday, no matter where I was in the world, we connected either in person or by Skype or phone at 5:00 a.m. Our sessions always began with meditation, so Jaime could gauge my quality of mind.

"Eastern people produce 30,000 thoughts per day, on average, so they are calmer and more patient," Jaime once told me. "Anglos produce 40,000 thoughts per day, which makes them more orderly and anal. We Latinos produce 60,000 thoughts every day. We're passionate, distracted but also extremely creative. Then there's you, Antonio. I believe you produce 70,000 thoughts each day. Stopping your mind is very difficult!"

During my first session after swimming in San Francisco Bay in June 2016, I confessed that I didn't think I could handle the cold water, and that I was destined for failure. He'd never seen me so sapped of self-confidence.

"The problem is not the cold water," he said, "It's your fear of the cold water. The cold water exists. It will always be there. We can't change that, but we can change how you relate to it, and how it affects you, so that's what we will do."

At first, I didn't understand what he was talking about. Could anybody really shatter the rules of thermodynamics? When human beings steep themselves in cold water for hours on end, their core temperature plummets. When the water temperature drops too low for too long, they will become hypothermic. That's how it works. Was Jaime suggesting I could regulate my body temperature from the inside out rather than the other way around? I was aware that martial arts and yoga masters had proven their ability to overcome the laws of nature before, but could a simple sinner like me do that? Could I defeat science? I doubted it very much, but I also knew I had to surrender to Jaime totally, and buy into his madness 100%, or I had no chance whatsoever of achieving my dream.

Over the next year, we tackled the problem by working on three techniques repeatedly. The first was to strengthen my focus, by separating myself from daily stress and difficulty in work and life. Jaime's theory was that because my mind was so preoccupied with business (by then I owned several) and my political network, that it was hard for me to sit still and focus my mind without doing something dynamic, like swimming, running or working out. The physical strain helped quell those thoughts and preoccupations, but as soon as I sat still my mind became the Lincoln tunnel, a high traffic zone.

Whenever I was in town, we met face to face, before dawn, in a common room in his steel and glass high rise apartment building in Santa Fe, a relatively new luxury neighborhood in Mexico City. It was sleek and modern with white tiled floors, dimmable recessed lighting and views overlooking a jigsaw of skyscrapers. He kept the lights low.

"Tell me about your week," he'd ask as I sat down on the leather sofa across from him. I'd express how everything was going with my training and at work. He'd listen, but not to the words alone. He also paid attention to the quality of my speech, if I held eye contact or if I stared to the heavens or the floor. He wanted to see how I reacted as I expressed myself. He wasn't the type to give me advice. He was too busy diagnosing my mind.

Then he would close his eyes, a cue for me to close mine. He breathed long, deep and slow, bringing a sense of quiet reverence to the space before leading me through qi gong movements to cleanse my energy and calm my mind. After that we practiced meditation to tune out useless thoughts.

259

"Keep the breath long and slow and count to ten, not out loud, but in your own mind," he said during one visit in the summer of 2016. "As soon as a thought pops into your brain, you must begin again at one." It's not easy to silence your mind. In fact, it's one of the most difficult challenges in life. It's a technique I've practiced intermittently over the years, and it can be a struggle, but whenever I'm engaged in an athletic quest, Jaime is always there to sharpen my skills. "Once you can count to ten, three times in a row with your eyes shut, and without any other thoughts piercing your mind, you can move on to twenty."

It took me weeks to get there. I'd practice for 15 minutes a day most mornings before I hit the pool, but eventually I did get to twenty and when I gave him the news he was very pleased because it signaled that I was ready for a new technique.

"I call this the pearl meditation," he said when he first introduced it to me. "They practice a version of it in Tibet where the Himalayan winters can be unbelievably cold. Monks use it when they sit in meditation, and the messengers use it on the trail as they run in sub-zero temperatures wearing just their robes. They keep themselves warm by creating a furnace in their belly with their own mind."

He sat opposite me and I watched him place his palm below his navel. "You have an energy center here, called the *tan tien*. Go ahead, place your palm below your navel." I did as he asked. "Now count your breaths and visualize a pearl in your belly at the same time." I began and after a few minutes of silence he spoke again. "Do you see it? Do you see a pearl?"

I nodded as I saw my imaginary pearl flicker to life in my mind's eye. With my eyes closed, my breath long, slow and deep, I kept concentrating on my core and soon the image in my head coalesced into a bright, round, gleaming and spinning pearl, the size of a large cobblestone.

"Very good. Let it glow red," he said, "as if it's a coal smoldering in a furnace. That's where I need your mind. Right here, right now, but also when you are in the water. You will swim, count your strokes, keep your mind blank, and focus on your red pearl. That will be your internal thermostat. The cold will be there, of course, but that's outside your control so you won't put your mind there. That's none of our business.

"Remember, you are not your problems and you are not your challenges. You are not the cold or the heat or success or failure. You are bigger than all of that. We all are. So, the less you identify with the cold, or any other struggle that has you in its grip, the easier it will be to endure.

"Everything is temporary. No matter what's going on in your life, no matter how cold the water, if you keep stoking the inner fire in your gut, feel that heat build, and let everything else go, you will arrive where you need to be."

I don't remember how long I sat in meditation that morning, but I do remember watching my spinning pearl glow red like coal. I gave it shape, color, and power, and in return it gave off waves of warm energy that rippled through my body from my inner core to the surface of my skin until a trickle of sweat snaked down from my forehead and dripped from the bridge of my nose. When I blinked my eyes open, seconds later, the sun had risen high above Mexico City, the room had warmed up like a fishbowl under a heat lamp, and Jaime was gone.

This swim, across the

most harrowing channel

in the Oceans Seven,

washed away all that

stale regret. It redeemed

me from all my failures

and shortcomings.

13

The North Channel

I'd been in the historic fishing village of Donaghadee in Northern Ireland for three weeks, and the weather 263 wasn't cooperating. If the sky was clear, the winds were howling. When the wind relented, the fog rolled in bringing with it low visibility and cool rain. None of this is unseasonal for August in Ireland, but if you're an open water swimmer with a marathon on the brain, it's a bit of a nightmare.

Much like the American Pacific Northwest, or the city of San Francisco, summer is fleeting along the North Channel—a narrow strait that separates the northeastern edge of Northern Ireland and the southwest coast of Scotland, and a maritime link that connects the Irish Sea with the North Atlantic Ocean. When the sun might choose to reveal itself or the wind stop blowing is anyone's guess, which is why swimmers like me book one-week weather windows in Donaghadee, hoping the Channel gods bestow an opportunity upon them. After months or even years of training, yet armed only with hope, we are prone to superstition as we consult satellite weather readings and attempt to decipher the fates.

My weather window officially opened on Saturday, July 29th, but for those first three days, thanks to swirling gales, swimming the channel was out of the question. My captain, Quinton Nelson, didn't like the weather reports for Monday either. He wasn't the type willing to take risks others might. According to the forecast on Wind Guru, the early hours on Tuesday looked great for a swim, but when I met with Quinton on Monday night, he remained circumspect.

Quinton was the prototypical salty dog. His clothes were faded, his skin weathered, his salt and pepper hair tousled, yet his demeanor was calm and unflappable. When he spoke, his words came slow but firm. I showed him Wind Guru's predictions and he shook me off.

"In the North Channel," he said in his thick brogue, "it's virtually impossible for any swimmer to make the crossing in winds above 10 knots. In all my years, I've never seen it done." Having wished for better news, I averted my eyes and stared from the pier out onto the open sea. "And yet," he continued, "there is nothing better looking forward in the week either, and it would be terrible if you returned to Mexico without being able to attempt the swim."

"Don't worry about that," I said. "Just give me your professional opinion in all candor."

"Let's keep monitoring it," he said.

We agreed to abandon any plans to swim the following morning and planned to meet again on Tuesday night. But when I woke up on Tuesday morning, the sky was clear and the wind still. After a brief 45-minute swim, Nora and I contemplated the seemingly perfect weather—the best we'd seen during our Donaghadee residency—and what looked like a missed opportunity. Our assumptions were confirmed when on the walk back to our inn after the swim, we learned that a South African swimmer had shoved off early that morning to attempt his crossing.

Quinton was being careful. Lucía appreciated that and I respected him, but it was difficult not to be frustrated and wonder if we hadn't lost our lone opportunity to swim that week. Nora was more upset than I was, but we both also knew that the North Channel is famous for its dynamic climate, and sure enough, the winds picked up at noon, just as Quinton suspected. Later that afternoon, we learned that after about six hours of suffering in the channel, the South African was pulled from the sea, and rushed to the hospital with hypothermia.

The possibility of hypothermia was the reason I'd postponed my North Channel attempt the year before. Since then, I'd made pilgrimage after pilgrimage to San Francisco to swim in cold water. With each ensuing visit, my tolerance grew bit by little bit, and when I was able to successfully cross the Catalina Channel in January 2017, that was a great sign, but it had been so difficult I knew I needed more exposure; more self-inflicted cold-water torture. So as the winter turned to spring, I continued to test myself.

Each time I dipped into the frigid, murky, neon green San Francisco Bay was an opportunity to tune deeper into the practices Jaime prescribed for me. My job was to relax

265

completely, even as the cold attempted to seize my muscles, seep into my bones, and dominate my psyche, while I worked to maintain the brisk pace necessary to achieve my goal of crossing a hypothermic channel before breaking down. That meant cultivating focus and visualizing the red pearl of energy in my navel; my imaginary smoldering coal, my internal heating system. During my Catalina swim, my heater was on the fritz. It blinked on and off as I suffered toward success. With just four weeks to go before my weather window would open in Northern Ireland, I landed in San Francisco for one last round of training and my last opportunity to perfect my technique.

We planned a series of four swims in four days in and around Aquatic Park. The year before, in June of 2016, the San Francisco Bay had laid me low. No matter how long I swam, whether it was 45 minutes or four hours, the cold would hit me like a sledgehammer in my gut and groin. The pain was monumental and nonstop, and after emerging from the sea, it would take over an hour for my core body temperature to recover enough for the pain to subside and longer even for my feet to feel close to normal. I'd been seen shivering on the Aquatic Park pier, my bones rattling uncontrollably, too many times to count. Yet through it all I gained in experience and confidence, and my fear of the cold faded as my abilities to withstand and push back against it had grown.

Over the course of those four days in July 2017, I swam a total of nine hours, including two swims of three and four hours each, in temperatures as low as 12.8°C. My body responded better than I'd hoped. It cooled without pain and I was able to maintain a steady, efficient rhythm. Afterwards,

I didn't need to sit in the sauna for 45 minutes to regain my core temperature as I had on my previous visits. I recovered quickly. All I needed was ten minutes in the sauna and I was back to myself. I'd become a cold-water marine mammal, insulated with brown fat, just in time to take on the most audacious swim challenge of my athletic career.

Before I left the South End Rowing Club for my flight across the Atlantic, I gathered sand from the beach at Aquatic Park and a jar of water from the Bay to bring with me to Northern Ireland, as a reminder of what I'd already done and was capable of doing. I'm not a superstitious person, but with the weather fraught and my chances at a crossing diminishing by the day, I felt the need to act. On Tuesday evening, August 1st, with just 72 hours left in my weather window, I gathered my team and friends from the local swim club, the Chunky Dunkers, for an impromptu pagan ceremony, hoping to convince the fates in my favor. I spilled the sand from Aquatic Park onto the beach and sprinkled water from both San Francisco Bay and Las Estacas—my twin training grounds—into the sea. With nearly two dozen fellow swimmers looking on, I asked the North Channel for permission to cross.

Early returns were not good. When I met with Quinton again on Tuesday night, he said the forecast for Wednesday, which had initially looked promising, had soured and that we would need to wait one more day. He didn't have to elaborate beyond that. I knew the situation. I was down to the very end of my weather window. My swim would launch on Thursday, August 3rd or I would have to wait at least one more calendar year.

I'd been in Donaghadee for three weeks by then. That gave me two weeks to acclimatize to the time zone and the water itself before my weather window. On my first morning in town, the wind howled at over 20 knots, but with a sheltered harbor a short walk from our inn, Pier 36, it was easy to find water smooth enough for a workout.

One of the things I love most about open water swimming are the views you get from the ocean. Glittering cities, rugged coastline, jade mountains, and small villages cobbled from brick and stone, all show their best angles to those blessed to view them from the open water. My repeated morning swims followed by long walks, terrific seafood lunches, and good single malt scotch unlocked a place in my heart for quirky, sweet Donaghadee.

Set about 29 kilometers east of Belfast, the town centers on its 17th century lighthouse and harbor, and its hillside Moat, a crenulated old fort. It has a quaint village feel and is home to fewer than 7000 people, but its proximity to a bustling city, and its working harbor, has fueled lasting prosperity. The best part is that a good chunk of the population either regularly swims in the North Channel or knows people who do thanks to the Chunky Dunkers, a legendary local swim crew.

The Dunkers' origin story centers on a local family who committed to swimming in the North Channel every day for a calendar year. They weren't going for speed or distance. Often, they didn't even swim freestyle. They just agreed to dare the cold for as little as ten or fifteen minutes before coming in to warm up. Often the swims lasted longer, but from the beginning they had but one sacred rule: no wetsuits. Although a small group of the Chunky Dunkers swim daily, the biggest swim day of their week is Sunday. On my first Sunday in town, we all swam together. Afterwards I spoke to them about my Oceans Seven quest and signed their registry. It was a terrific honor and a joy to meet new friends with a shared passion.

For two weeks I swam for 90 minutes at least once and sometimes twice a day. The North Channel was a bit colder than the Pacific, but each successive swim brought less pain. I grew accustomed to numbness in my fingers and the raw gnaw of the cold on my mind. I relaxed and tuned into that red pearl, visualizing waves of heat emanating from my core and saturating my skin. On my walk back to the inn, I enjoyed smiles and waves from familiar faces. I was acclimatizing to the sea and to Donaghadee, and it seemed the village had acclimated to me in return.

I'd brought all the usual suspects with me for this final swim: Ricardo and Rafa, Pablo, Lucía and Ximena, Nora, Ariadna and Joaquín, and Brad. We reserved all five rooms at Pier 36, and the owners, Margaret and Denis Waterworth, never failed to make us feel at home. They understood athletes well. After all, their son Lewis was a nine-time Ironman and his brother Jody was a record-breaking water ski jumper.

They introduced me to local legends like Lynton Mortensen, an Australian who in 2017 swam both the North Channel and English Channel two weeks apart, and Padraig Mallon, a North Channel finisher. Padraig also charters his own boat to help swimmers achieve their North Channel dreams. When we met, he lamented that his playground, while perhaps the most difficult of all the Oceans Seven, is also the most overlooked. He understood the reasons. The weather is so bad that many swims get called off before the boat ever has a chance to leave the harbor. Plus, the cold is so severe, even great swimmers have a hard time enduring the ten, twelve, or even fourteen hours it may take to swim from Northern Ireland to Scotland.

Then there's the lion's mane jellyfish, the largest of all jellies, a translucent tangerine beauty with a painful sting. The North Channel is known for vast blooms of them. On her North Channel swim, my friend Kim Chambers was stung hundreds of times. She staggered out of the water in Scotland swollen, hypothermic and delirious. She barely remembers the aftermath of her triumphant swim and was forced to "celebrate" her triumph in the hospital.

Put that all together and it's no surprise that while the English Channel has been crossed over 2,400 times (solos and relays combined), upon my arrival in Donaghadee only 47 people had successfully made the North Channel crossing. And as the sun set on Wednesday August 2nd, 2017, it was unlikely I'd have the opportunity to try and become the 48th. When he arrived at Pier 36 that night, Quinton looked glum.

"I feel very sorry about this," he said, "but right now, I'm not seeing the conditions." He paused. I felt the sting of disappointment but didn't say a word. "Of course, the weather can change, and if you are willing to go to bed tonight knowing there might be a possibility..." He arched an eyebrow. I smiled in return. He put his palms on the table and shrugged. "I can't promise anything, but let's meet here at 7:00 in the morning and decide."

Perhaps if I knew for sure that we would swim on Thursday, the anticipation would have made sleep difficult, and though my dream hung in the balance like so many clouds in the sky, I had no control, which was liberating. There was absolutely nothing I could do about my predicament and with the pressure off, I fell asleep before 9:00 p.m. and slept soundly until my alarm blared at 5:00 a.m.

I rose quickly and with coffee in hand, left the inn for a walk. The streets were damp from rain the night before, and the sky was overcast and gray. Things didn't look much different than they had for the past three weeks, so I made my mind up that if Quinton decided a crossing was impossible given the conditions, I would ask for at least six hours of swimming. I wanted to taste the wilds of the North Channel with my body and mind to give me something to contemplate and analyze in case I had to return at some later date to finish the job.

After meditating and doing some qi gong, I met Rafa at 6:20 a.m., as planned, and we began my stretching routine as if the swim was a go. Quinton found us there, finishing my warm up, when he arrived at 7:00 a.m.

"The situation is very difficult," he said as he looked toward the open sea. "The weather is bad now, as you can see. But in three or four hours, according to the reports, it may improve." His gaze found me. We locked eyes. "It's your swim, Antonio. You have the last word."

"Do you trust that it will improve?" I asked.

"Yes," he said. That was the word I'd been hoping to hear since my weather window opened. All I'd ever wanted was one opportunity. I extended my hand and he shook it.

"Let's go to Scotland," I said.

With the sky still dark gray and drizzly, we strolled to the marina where I kissed Ximena on the cheek, hugged my brother Brad who would stay behind as well, and took Lucía into my arms for a farewell embrace. All of us were giddy, buzzing with opportunity and anticipation, yet still concerned because the quilt of heavy clouds looked foreboding as they spread over the grey-green sea.

I was the last of my team to climb aboard the *James and Frances Macfarlane*, a 16-meter former rescue boat. Within seconds, Quinton took the helm and we shoved off, motoring out of the harbor, toward the starting point. As we skimmed the rippled surface, Ariadna and Nora applied the usual layer of zinc oxide and petroleum jelly to every inch of my exposed skin and prepared me for the journey to come.

Ten minutes later, with the boat idling, I leapt into the sea and swam for shore. The water felt surprisingly warm. It was still a chilly 13°C, but over the past weeks I'd become used to swimming in 12°C water and even that modest increase felt like a gift. I eased toward shore, where a rocky green slope degraded into black rock scree that met the ocean, and emerged onto the rocks in my Speedo, goggles and a custom swim cap designed for the occasion. I waved and my team gave me the sign, but I didn't set off right away. I knew the way forward would demand everything I had, but I also suspected that my success would not depend upon my abilities alone. I'd need some good fortune and calm conditions. I needed a cooperative sea. So, I took a moment to connect with the channel and asked for permission to cross from Ireland to

Portpatrick, Scotland, 35 kilometers away. After that, there was but one thing left to do. At 7:30 a.m. on August 3rd, 2017, I started to swim.

I kept a modest early pace of 60 strokes per minute as the Irish coast faded into the fog behind me. Rain continued to fall, but the wind was light, which gave me hope. In the third hour the clouds peeled back, revealing swatches of blue and an elegant rainbow. With the sun on my shoulders, I found a more efficient rhythm and picked up my pace to 62, then 64 strokes per minute. I also got my first glimpse of the Scottish shore. It was still far off, and a bit fuzzy, but it was no longer a distant dream. It was right there waiting for me.

Although the first recorded attempt to swim the North Channel dates back to 1928, it wasn't until after World War II, on July 27th, 1947, when the English war hero Tom Blower made the first successful crossing in 15 hours and 26 minutes. His record stood for over 20 years. There were several attempts made in the 1950s and 1960s, but none were successful, and at least one swimmer died from hypothermia after being pulled from the water by his support team.

Kevin Murphy, another English swim legend, was the first to duplicate Blower's feat when on September 11th, 1970 he made the crossing in just 11 hours and 21 minutes. He did it again the following year, though it took him over three hours longer. No matter, that second swim made him the first to cross the channel twice, a list that remains laughably short, which speaks to the swim's extraordinary difficulty.

On August 22nd, 1988, American Alison Streeter became the first woman to swim the channel, making the crossing in a record-breaking nine hours and 54 minutes, an overall record that held for decades. Streeter would go on to swim the channel twice more. She and Kevin Murphy, who made a third crossing 17 years after his first, are two of only three swimmers to complete a solo North Channel swim on three separate occasions.

As I attempted to swim my way to a more modest place in history, I kept waiting for the venomous lion's mane jellyfish to surface, but they were nowhere to be found. The cold was ever-present and daunting, but like a Tibetan messenger flung out into the Himalayan winter, my relaxed focus was exactly where it needed to be. I counted my strokes, visualized that glowing red pearl and kept my demons at bay. As usual, I stopped for sips of water and a feed of Accel Gel every 30 minutes, and by 2:00 p.m., I was over halfway across the channel, an hour ahead of schedule, and loving every bit of it.

Looking back, during my other channel swims, my mind was always tethered to some nagging preoccupation or unforeseen obstacle. Unpredictable currents, schools of jellyfish, rogue container ships, fear of injury, and, of course, the future, all acted as a drag, draining my strength and slowing me down. From the beginning, the biggest bogeyman of my entire Oceans Seven journey had been this gloomy stretch of sea. For three years, the North Channel had haunted me, in and out of the water, yet here I was in the middle it, and I was actually enjoying myself.

Of course, no channel crossing comes easy and the weather

proved as dynamic as advertised. It seemed to change every 30 minutes. There was sun, then rain, then a bit of wind, and then it was calm. The air temperature dipped and spiked, but through it all, I stayed on rhythm, focused on each stroke, each moment, keeping my mind as blank as possible.

The most challenging hour of swimming in my entire life was the most absorbing experience I've ever had in or out of the water.

That was the key. I had to keep my mind on a tight leash. I couldn't think ahead because I knew that anticipation only sparks more thoughts, which attach to emotions, and emotions often swirl into anxiety. Plus, if this was to be my final swim, I wanted to savor every last stroke. That meant staying single minded, and truly feeling every one of them.

And yet, at my 4:00 p.m. feed, Nora couldn't contain

her excitement. She leaned over the railing, and shouted, "Antonio, you are just two hours away! We are so close!" Her delight was infectious, and I became emotional, smiling through unexpected tears, as I sucked down my water and energy gel. This journey had required so much faith and hard work, more than I'd ever imagined. I'd received unending support from my brothers, Lucía, Ximena, and David. I'd been embraced by communities and fellow swimmers all over the world and was supported by the best coaching staff on the open water. And I was just two hours away from completing what I'd imagined would be a nightmare swim but had morphed into a beautiful dream.

In other words, my mental discipline was not where it needed to be. I'd relaxed too much. Instead of working to finish what I started, I was acting as if my success was already guaranteed. That's a rookie move. In the open ocean, two hours is plenty of time for disaster to strike. Especially in the North Channel, where conditions are known to deteriorate in the flap of a seagull's wing.

I felt the shift in the current almost immediately after that feed. I went from moving freely to being held in place. I was hammering at a 62 stroke-per-minute pace and felt like I was moving backward. So, I swam harder, but still I did not move. An hour passed, and I'd gained no ground at all. I was still two hours away. Or was I?

Back on the boat, Mark Hamilton, the official observer, consulted his charts. The tide was shifting, meaning that negative current would only grow in strength. The tides change every six hours, and though I was as well prepared for the cold water as any swimmer could be, this was not Hawaii, and the likelihood of a successful North Channel crossing of over 18 hours was not high. At my next feed, Nora gave me the bad news.

"Quinton said you have about an hour to break through." I flashed to the first conversation I ever had with Quinton at his marina.

"The hardest thing is to actually get to Scotland," he had said. "Many swims have been suspended meters from the coast."

At the time, I remember thinking that would be the absolute worst-case scenario and now it was happening to me. Rafa, sensing my weakness of mind, my drift toward self pity, leaned over the side of the boat with fire in his eyes.

"Pick up your pace, Toño! It's time to go! Balls out!"

Damn right. I tossed the water bottle into the net, and got to work, raising my pace to 65 strokes a minute. That wasn't good enough, so I cranked it up even harder. My team cheered me on. They chanted, sang and screamed, sending their encouragement onto the wings of the Scottish wind. It was exactly what I needed to keep fighting.

I hammered away at the shifting tides, trying to chop the channel down to size, centimeter by precious centimeter. I reached 67 strokes per minute, then 68. My lungs heaved, my eyes welled with tears, my heart pounded. If I was making any progress, I could not tell.

I was deep in a flow state. I'd become a speck of consciousness in a vast, undulating sea. I was an open-hearted pilgrim, a sinner weighed down with dreams and desires, absorbing the energy of the ocean and the whole cosmos. Then, with each breath, I used that energy to forge my way through a wall of resistance in order to reach my promised land.

The channel gave me everything it had, and with focused determination, I gave it all back and asked for more. Thirty minutes passed in the blink of an eye. I stopped for my feed, then dropped back into my zone and did it all over again. The most challenging hour of swimming in my entire life was the most absorbing experience I've ever had in or out of the water. Then, all of a sudden, it was over.

I'd broken through. Progress was palpable. Scotland moved toward me with open arms, but this time I didn't stop. There would be no more premature celebrations, and no more water breaks. Not with Quinton's words from our first meeting still echoing in my brain.

"You never know when the currents will go against you... you never know..."

I kept swimming hard, but the North Channel was done toying with me. I'd proven myself a worthy pirate and my dream was about to come true. There would be one final hurdle, however. As we approached the craggy coastline that is Portpatrick, I removed my goggles and saw the beach for what it was, a jumble of jagged boulders thrashed with surf. There was no safe place to land. I asked for some guidance. Quinton shrugged.

"You have to swim to those rocks," he said.

I nodded, rolled my eyes, and laughed. Then did as I was told. As I entered the impact zone, a wave broke behind me, rolled over me, and flipped me sideways. All I could do was extend my exhausted arms and weakened legs as flat and wide as a starfish and hope not to smash into a boulder, face first. My right hand grazed shallow rocks, and I managed to grab an edge to pull myself into a seated position on top of a flat, wide boulder as the tide washed out. I caught my breath, and looked behind, above, and all around me. This was Scotland. I'd made it.

Three times in my life I'd been so well prepared for a swim event. The first two were the Pan American trials in 1974 and the Olympic trials in 1976. Both of those ended in failure. I never did achieve my childhood dreams, but this swim, across the most harrowing channel in the Oceans Seven, washed away all that stale regret. It redeemed me from all my failures and shortcomings.

The North Channel Swimming Association doesn't require a toes dry finish. You simply have to touch the rocky shore. According to Mark Hamilton, I'd done that just before 9:00 p.m., with the last shards of pale light still lingering in the summer sky. After a swim of 13 hours 32 minutes and 32 seconds, I became the seventh swimmer in history to achieve the Oceans Seven. I was 58 years old, the oldest to ever do it.

Quinton sounded his horn.

I raised my left arm high.

Embrace life,

cultivate discipline,

and you will be

better equipped

to savor the

present and enjoy

your journey.

14

Enjoy the Journey

Standing in the shadows, on the wings of the stage, butterflies fluttered inside me for the first time in years. It wasn't the glare that shook me. I love the spotlight, and enjoy speaking to crowds, but this event was different than all the others. This one was special.

I was backstage at Stanford's historic Memorial Auditorium, one of my alma mater's landmark buildings. It was late 2017 and I was about to speak to my classmates at our 35-year reunion. Brad Howe was there, of course, alongside Lucía, our son David and his fiancée Itzi (Ximena had final exams back in Boston). All of them were tucked into a sea of old friends and peers.

I wasn't nervous due to lack of preparation. I was set to deliver a speech about my Oceans Seven swims, and all the challenges I faced along the way. It was the kind of speech I'd been giving for several weeks. The content didn't make me nervous at all. It was the context.

Perspiration beaded on my forehead and my palms became clammy, as I flashed on the first time I'd been asked to speak at length in front my peers at Stanford. It was my sophomore year. I still considered myself a Marxist and enrolled in a Marx seminar taught by a legendary professor. There were only eight students in the class, every one of them brilliant and always well prepared. Worse, each time we handed in an essay, the professor made us read it aloud, and defend it like a dissertation to our fellow students.

Just imagine what it felt like for me, a young Mexican still perfecting his English, to read in front of a collection of well-read, self-assured Stanford students. I felt like an imposter, and each time I was asked to read my work, it was painful because my performance was pitiful. Now, here I was, one of the keynote speakers of the reunion, and I could see one or two of those faces in the crowd. I couldn't have scripted it in my wildest imagination.

In many ways, I was still riding the high of the North Channel. The evening of the swim we buzzed back to the marina and enjoyed a feast for the ages at Harbour & Company, the sister restaurant to Pier 36. We dined on fresh seafood, drank several bottles of Spanish wine and enough single malt to support a small distillery, until my team demanded sleep in the wee hours of the morning. I wandered back to my room with Lucía too but couldn't sleep. I was still buzzing with adrenaline and accomplishment. So, I left the inn and strolled the seaside, entranced by the channel. Periodically, I closed my eyes and flashed back to all the others too. The

Oceans Seven, what an adventure it had been. I felt fortunate, but it was fortune I'd worked for, which gave me a deep sense of peace and satisfaction.

Although the news of my swim spread through the open-water-swim community fairly quickly, it took a few days before the story broke mainstream. And the fact that it did was its own stroke of luck I never envisioned. Most open-water-swim stories never latch on to the news cycle at all, but in the spring of 2017, I'd had the pleasure of speaking with an independent American reporter in advance of a swim Kim Chambers and I led from San Diego to Tijuana. It was part Trump protest march and part solidarity swim, demonstrating the fraternity of two great nations that rely on one another and always will. He wrote that story for *Outside* magazine, but during our interview I mentioned my Oceans Seven quest, and he said he would follow up on my progress in the coming weeks. Two months passed, and I never heard from him.

So, I was surprised when his message found me during my Donaghadee residency. We spoke a few times before and again after I swam the North Channel. When the article was published the following Sunday, it wasn't in *Outside*. It was the cover story in *The New York Times'* Sunday Sports section. We had top billing above Usain Bolt. If you would have told me that would happen, I'd have called you a liar. An open water swimmer few had ever heard of getting more ink than the greatest sprinter in history? Even today that sounds crazy. But it happened.

That publicity came with aftershocks of still more publicity throughout Mexico and around the world. I was on national TV back home, in papers around the world and eventually it won me an invitation to address my high achieving classmates, but with minutes to go before I took the stage at Stanford, I found myself in an existential spin cycle, second guessing my material. What was the point of it all, I wondered? Did my Oceans Seven swim actually matter in the grand scheme of things? Was achievement for achievement's sake worth anything at all? These are exactly the sort of questions you should avoid at all costs before any stage performance. This is the stuff panic attacks are made of.

For decades, I'd lived by the sage mantra of any competitive athlete. The past is over with, and the future does not exist. All we have is the present moment. Yet so many of us are so tangled up with regret, ambition, depression, or victimization, that it becomes difficult to enjoy the present. Sometimes, that's circumstantial. Life can be hard and intimidating. We don't get everything we want, and many have trouble even finding what they need to live with dignity and security. Other times, our anxiety, our lack of enjoyment, is a result of subconscious choices. We are choosing to absorb the sound and fury that is the present moment in a particular way which may be at odds with where we hope or wish our life is or was going, which leads to a feeling of victimhood and loss.

Standing backstage, I tried to force my mind back to the script I'd already memorized, the one describing my "life's greatest achievement". But could any swim or collection of swims really be the greatest achievement of anyone's life? There had to be more to life than that. Should I scrap the swim speech altogether, and instead focus on the importance of relationships?

CHAPTER FOURTEEN

I thought about my brothers, how we started in business so young to help my parents cover our school fees. All four of us Argüelles brothers have remained close our entire lives and because of that we've all enjoyed success. Diego has proven to be a sharp entrepreneur his entire adult life and remains my business partner; Raúl has enjoyed a long tenure as a top executive at multinational companies; finally, my youngest brother, Arturo, is an accomplished restauranteur. We all have happy families and we continually invest in and support one another.

The same is true for Brad. My strange American brother completely wasted his Stanford education and opted to become an artist. Good thing he's a genius. His canvasses and sculpture adorn my home, as well as galleries and even museums. I take pride in Brad's success because I was there when he was struggling. I've witnessed his grace and perseverance too many times to count, most recently when he lost his home and art studio (along with priceless works in progress) during the Malibu fires in 2018. But losing so much didn't seem to bother him. Through loss he remained, and remains, in gratitude. What an example he is. I'm so grateful to have him in mine and my children's lives.

My eyes panned to Lucía, who couldn't see me watching her. I'd married the love of my life, a successful Lacanian psychoanalyst, and we helped each other raise beautiful children. Ximena recently finished her MBA and is poised for a career in social enterprise, while David also recently earned his PhD from Stanford.

I remain close with former President Zedillo, Miguel Limón, and Jaime Serra, who has enjoyed a comeback of

285

his own. These days, he runs a think tank and helps shape economic policy in Mexico and around the world. When Trump railed against NAFTA during the 2016 presidential campaign, Serra's star rose again in Mexico. After all, he negotiated the dreaded deal.

Yes, when it comes to relationships, my wealth is beyond measure, but like high achievements, the health of our closest relationships doesn't always add up to a fulfilling life. Even those of us with every advantage, including the gift of love and friendship, can fail to see unexpected events as opportunities. We may miss out on important lessons and a deeper, existential fulfillment. We may become hopeless and depressed.

Waiting in the wings, there was no question that I felt fulfilled, but it wasn't because of the things I'd done or the people I loved. The secret to my success in work, sports, and life as a whole has been my ability to find joy and hope, and to remain open to unexpected opportunities as life unfolds moment by moment. That's not as easy as it sounds and it's a lesson I've had to learn and relearn over and over again.

The best example of that isn't in my swims, but in the later stages of my career as public servant, when I fell into education against my will. I never anticipated working at Conalep, and didn't much want to, but by the end, I didn't want to leave. So, I started my own school system, using the curriculum we created and perfected at Conalep, to continue to serve students in the outskirts of Mexico City. I've also continued to consult for public school systems in three Mexican states. I would never have guessed on my first day on the job in Metepec that education would become a passion that would fulfill me personally and financially for more than two decades, but it has because I was open to it. I was open to life, and I seized that opportunity with hard work.

I'll concede that it's easier to remain alert to opportunities if you command your own schedule. I was in charge at Conalep, so I didn't have to kowtow to an on-site supervisor. I had bosses, but our day-to-day contact was minimal. Obviously, most jobs don't allow for that. Our bosses request that we report at a given hour and we had better be there ready to get the job done. That kind of thing still happens to me from time to time. But your supervisors don't live in your head, and they are not in charge of how you think or how hard you work. You are.

Showing up to do your work is your choice, not theirs. Whenever possible, everything we engage in should be seen through the lens of choice. We choose how we feel and what we plan to do with our time every second of every day. We certainly choose the level of effort we bring, and if you look at life that way, you can't help but feel free.

Of course, freedom can be its own trap if it's not paired with self-discipline. Mexico has learned that. Overall, NAFTA has done wonders for our economy. It hasn't been perfect. Wages have not risen as high and prosperity hasn't been as equitably shared as we all hoped, but Mexico is clearly better off for engaging in the global marketplace.

At the same time, we haven't met those new opportunities and greater economic freedom with discipline when it comes to our diets. American fast-food brands seized on our open borders in the 1990s and have become institutions in

Mexico with disastrous health consequences. Childhood obesity has skyrocketed along with high blood pressure and heart disease.

Freedom without discipline is a recipe for disaster, and it always has been.

In 2016 my friend Steven Munatones, the founder of the World Open Water Swimming Association, survived a severe heart attack. His son acted fast, delivered CPR and brought him back to life. He was in a coma for a week and in the ICU for two weeks. Yet despite all that, or perhaps because of it, he remains optimistic and full of life at 57 years old, and he has a wonderful question he asks those he hasn't seen in a while. It's a question that he asks himself all the time.

"Where will you be swimming in 2050?"

I love that question because having an adventure in mind, a goal on the calendar, stimulates discipline. It's not about the outcome. Success and failure are all too fleeting. The best thing about setting big goals is that it makes daily life so much more interesting, challenging and fun.

In the early stages of my endurance sports career, I used to get depressed after completing an Ironman or a marathon swim. Having a mission to prepare for brought focus and a healthy discipline to my life and when it was over, I could feel that black hole open up beneath me again. These days, I don't have that same sense of depression or alienation after a swim, but I still try to have the next big thing queued up because I know that discipline is what turns freedom—of movement and mind, that sense that anything and everything is possible—into fulfillment.

Adventure and athletics demand the type of intellectual and physical rigor that invigorates our lives. They infuse each moment with meaning and vitality. Goals force us to push ourselves to become our best selves, and to me that's what this life is all about.

Often, I'm working on more than one big project, living more than one mission at a time. These days I'm part of a coalition working to address Mexico's current public health challenges. I brought a successful swim-a-thon, Swim for Your Heart, to Mexico. It's a week-long event in which tens of thousands of people around the country swim one kilometer each to raise awareness around the importance of physical activity and heart health.

As for childhood obesity, I've also created a curriculum with Rafa, called the ABCs of Mobility, to empower teachers in Mexican schools to get their students moving within and outside the classroom. We love our food in Mexico, but we need to be more physically fit too, and it has become a mission of mine to spread that gospel.

Another recent project I am very excited about is Brazada Abrazada, because it combines my two passions: swimming and education. I know that spending time in the pool can change a kid's life—it changed mine—and now I want other children to have the same opportunity I had. Through swimming and other aquatic activities, we want kids to receive holistic education and adopt healthy lifestyles. We started with two hundred children from the Colonel J. Cruz Gálvez boarding school, located in Hermosillo, Sonora, and, so far, we have managed to add 1,500 participants throughout the state.

And I'm still swimming, of course. For the joy of it, but also to prove that even at 60 years old, I'm not done pushing myself. Now that I've successfully swum seven of the world's great channels, there's only one thing left to do: Double down!

In August 2019, I swam my first Catalina double crossing. That's a 64.6-kilometer swim, from the California mainland to Catalina Island and back, and it took me 24 hours, 17 minutes and 49 seconds. It was the longest I'd ever been in the open water, and yet it was merely a prelude to an even greater challenge, a double crossing of the English Channel, currently on the calendar for summer 2020. My very first crossing of the English Channel was supposed to be a double. Imagine if I manage to achieve at age 61 what I couldn't do in my 40s. The possibility alone excites me, so does the challenge because it demands daily discipline.

Not long ago, I was in La Paz, training in the Gulf of California for eight hours at a time. Somewhere in the middle of the blue a giant fish approached me. Its dorsal fin broke the surface ten feet away and my heart plummeted into my gut. It was a shark alright, a big one. It was over six meters long, but as it swam closer, my fear faded into laughter. This shark wasn't dangerous. It didn't even have sharp teeth. It was a whale shark, and whale sharks are filter feeders. The gentle beauty swam toward me in regal silence, passed under me with its usual entourage of smaller fish trailing after it, before disappearing into the everlasting blue.

Those are the moments I live for.

Life is not about victories. Its beauty can be found in the

softer, deeper experiences that happen along the way, and the more often we remain open to opportunity, set goals and cultivate discipline, the more likely it is that beauty, joy and fulfillment will find us. That's the message I brought with me onto the Memorial Auditorium stage that night in 2017. Embrace life, cultivate discipline, and you will be better equipped to savor the present, and enjoy your journey.

When my name was called, I didn't move right away. As the applause reached its crescendo, Lucía craned her neck, and her searching eyes found me in the shadows, smiling, taking it all in. I looked over. She crossed her lovely legs, winked and gestured toward the center of the empty stage.

I stepped into the light.

ACKNOWLEDGEMENTS

The successful completion of a journey is rarely the achievement of a single person. I want to thank all those without whose support I would not have been able to reach the other shore.

My mother, for having instilled in me determination and the love for a job well done.

My father, for giving me the advice that allowed me to navigate through the storms.

Lucía, for being by my side and being the solid ground to which I always return.

Ximena, David and Itzi, for accompanying me in my dreams.

My brothers Diego, Raúl, Arturo, and Brad, for supporting me and encouraging me to do my best and never give up.

My teachers Mrs. Muñiz, Maricarmen Palacios, Miss Silins, Rusell Berman, and Jaime Serra, who, with much effort and dedication, got me to learn something.

Manuel Ángel Núñez, Enrique Escalante, Jaime Serra, Ernesto Zedillo, and Miguel Limón, who were not bosses, but patient mentors who helped me grow.

Alejandro Martí, Daniel Servitje, Claudio X. González Laporte, and Guillermo González Guajardo, for their generosity and faith in my projects.

My coaches Gabriel Altamirano, Nelson Vargas, Dick Beaver, Don Jacklin, Jim Gaughran, Rodolfo Aznar, Nora Toledano, Rafael Álvarez, Ricardo Durón, Ricardo González, and Héctor Chávez, for believing in me, in spite of my limitations.

Hermes Ilarraza, Ariadna del Villar and Radamés Ortiz, for giving me the medical care that allowed my body to continue swimming.

Quinton Nelson, Mark Hamilton, Mike Oram, Philip Rush, Jeff Kozlovich, Steve Haumschild, Michael Twigg-Smith, Captain Mizushima, Dan Simonelli, and Rafael Gutiérrez, for guiding me through the seven seas.

Karina López, Javier and Ramón Reverté, Fernando Gómez del Campo, Mara Garbuno, and Chris Hill, for helping me bring this story to life.

María Paula Martínez, Pablo Argüelles, and Paulo Nunes dos Santos, for capturing the landscapes and emotions of each adventure with their lenses.

Steven Munatones, for giving life to the Oceans Seven.

Adam Skolnick, for putting on paper the stories on which this story is based.

Franco Bavoni, for his excellent translation into Spanish and the tireless work of making sure that words are properly used, and Mauricio Tenorio, for his suggestions and help in nuancing a few passages.

Guillermina Velázquez, for always getting me out of everyday trouble.

José Luis Peña, for his unconditional support and the signs of friendship he has given me over so many years.

Sport City, for supporting athletes like myself and for offering me an aquatic oasis in the middle of a concrete jungle.

Las Estacas and all those who have made me feel at home in this natural paradise.

The ocean, for always receiving me with open arms. My heart belongs to it.